SIR EDMUND HILLARY

& The People of Everest

SIR EDMUND HILLARY
& The People of Everest

Foreword by
↣ HRH PRINCE PHILIP, DUKE OF EDINBURGH ↤

With Photographs by Anne B. Keiser
Text by Cynthia Russ Ramsay

A PROJECT OF
THE EXCELLENCE FOUNDATION

Andrews McMeel
Publishing

Kansas City

Sir Edmund Hillary & The People of Everest

Copyright © 2002 The Excellence Foundation
Design and Compilation Copyright © 2002 Lionheart Books, Ltd.

ISBN: 0-7407-2950-0
Library of Congress Cataloging-in-Publication Data on file

Sir Edmund Hillary & The People of Everest
was produced by
Lionheart Books, Ltd.
5105 Peachtree Industrial Boulevard
Atlanta, GA 30341

This book is a project of

THE EXCELLENCE FOUNDATION

For more information please see page 171.

SIR EDMUND HILLARY: EVEREST AND BEYOND
Celebrating the Life and Achievements of a Great New Zealander

Auckland **Museum**
Te Papa Whakahiku

Design: Carley Wilson Brown

ATTENTION: SCHOOLS AND BUSINESSES
Andrews McMeel books are available at quantity discounts with bulk purchase for educational,
business, or sales promotional use. For information, please write to: Special Sales Department,
Andrews McMeel Publishing, 4520 Main Street, Kansas City, MO 64111.

✤ TABLE OF CONTENTS ✤

On the occasion of the 50th anniversary of Edmund Hillary's triumphant ascent of Mount Everest on May 29, 1953, *Sir Edmund Hillary & The People of Everest* is dedicated with deep respect and admiration to "Sir Ed." This book celebrates Hillary's extraordinary life of achievement and honors his decades of unprecedented humanitarian work with the Sherpa people of Nepal. Working side by side with his Himalayan friends, Hillary's compassionate approach to community development has ultimately enabled the extraordinary Sherpa people to respond effectively to the significant challenges in their lives and the lives of their children.

GOLDEN ANNIVERSARY
Conquest of Mount Everest

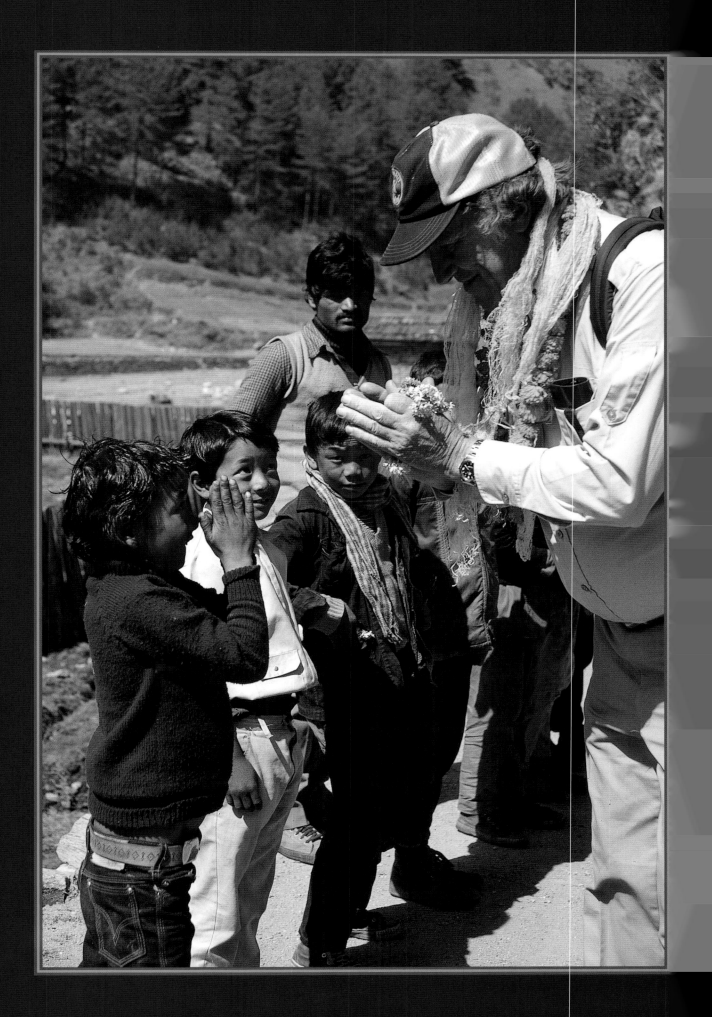

BUCKINGHAM PALACE.

On 2 June 1953, the day of the Coronation, the Queen and I were woken with the news that Hillary and Tenzing had reached the summit of Mount Everest. It was a marvellous beginning to a wonderful day.

For many people, reaching the summit of Everest would have been the apex of their career. Not so Edmund Hillary. The experience naturally transformed his life, but it gave it an unexpected twist. He could not avoid becoming a world-renowned "personality," but it was his affection for and devotion to the Sherpa people which directed and inspired the future course of his life. It would be difficult to exaggerate the value of his thoughtful and sensitive contribution to their welfare and to the conservation of their way of life in the spectacular Himalayan environment.

I am delighted that this book has been written. I hope it will inspire many others to follow his example of service to others and his deep concern for the natural environment.

HRH, Prince Philip, Duke of Edinburgh

Mount Everest had been in news headlines long before the first ascent by Edmund Hillary in 1953. And after that accomplishment, dramatic stories of summit attempts have continued to be featured in the news, especially after the 1996 tragedies. Yet hidden in Everest's shadow is the ongoing story of one man's efforts to improve the lives of the Sherpa people who live in the Solo Khumbu region of Nepal. It is the story of Sir Edmund Hillary's humanitarian work after his famous ascent, a chapter of his life he considers to be the most rewarding and satisfying of all.

I first met Hillary in May 1983. A photographer for *National Geographic*, I had traveled to Nepal to work with a film crew that was making a documentary to celebrate the 30th anniversary of his ascent of Everest with Tenzing Norgay Sherpa on May 29, 1953. I reached my destination in Khumbu late one May afternoon. Standing outside Hillary's tent in the village of Khunde, I felt a little anxious about meeting "Sir Ed."

Soon the tent flap opened, and a large, broad-shouldered man emerged, clad in khaki pants and an Icelandic sweater I would come to know well during the years ahead. It was a daunting sight until his broad smile greeted my eyes. His warm and gracious welcome was a wonderful beginning to what would become a twenty-year working relationship and friendship.

Return to Everest, the *National Geographic* documentary that we were filming, told the story of Hillary's remarkable humanitarian work with the Sherpa people, an effort largely unknown to the greater public. The film also described the creation of Sagarmatha (Mt. Everest) National Park, the park that had been created, with Hillary's help, to preserve the fragile environment in the Solo Khumbu region.

I spent the next few weeks photographing Hillary and the Sherpas in their Solo Khumbu homeland beneath the spectacular Himalayan peaks. What struck me most was the remarkable mutual admiration and trust that existed between Hillary and the Sherpa people, and I wanted to learn more about the origin of Hillary's humanitarian efforts. I discovered that, on one of several trips to Khumbu after his Everest success, Hillary gathered a group of close Sherpa friends and asked if, in return for their service to him during his climbing expeditions, there were some way he could be of assistance to them. "Our children have eyes, but they cannot see," they answered. "We need a school in Khumjung." Hillary's perceptive response was, "Together we shall build a school." As a result, he created the Himalayan Trust and began to devote much of his life in service to his Sherpa friends.

In the years that followed, Hillary helped the Sherpa community build twenty-six schools for Sherpa children, two major hospitals, a number of village health clinics, and the first central water systems in many villages. He also helped build new bridges and create more accessible routes between villages. And in later years when the Khumbu environment was threatened by deforestation and trash problems, Hillary helped establish programs to address these concerns. Eventually, Hillary hoped, the Sherpas would take leadership roles in their own communities to continue the health, education, and conservation efforts he had helped initiate.

Transformed by what I experienced on my first trip to Solo Khumbu, I vowed that I would find a way to return to this enchanting region and make my own personal contribution. The opportunity came in 1985 when Hillary welcomed my offer to return to Nepal to photograph his Himalayan Trust projects. As a result, in the years that followed, I had the opportunity to participate in several "Hillary Treks."

The Hillary Trek seemed to follow its own unique and delightful format. Typically, when Hillary would arrive in a region, a group of Sherpas would emerge out of nowhere, decorate

Hillary with *katas* (white blessing scarves) and rhododendron leis, and bestow thermoses of local brew on our party. After much conviviality, a Sherpa who could read would unfold a crumpled piece of paper and deliver a petition to Hillary. Hillary always listened closely and gave every request careful consideration, but he felt it was critical that the Sherpas take ownership over the projects they requested. In this way, he helped them preserve their sense of self-respect and cultural identity. But once a project was approved, Hillary was always an on-site participant, personally involved in every step of each undertaking.

As I began to accumulate a collection of photographs and to befriend a number of key players in this saga, the idea of a photographic essay on Hillary's life of service began to take shape. However, I couldn't separate Hillary's life from that of the Sherpas. Just as Hillary had wished, certain Sherpas who had been students in the first schools he had helped to establish were assuming leadership roles of significant responsibility: Mingma Norbu Sherpa, the first Sherpa warden of Sagarmatha National Park, who now is an executive with the World Wildlife Fund in Washington, D.C.; Ang Rita Sherpa, Executive Director of Hillary's Himalayan Trust in Kathmandu, Nepal; Lhakpa Norbu Sherpa, an executive with the Mountain Institute in Nepal, and currently working in Tibet; Mingma Gyelzen and Kami Temba, both Sherpa doctors; and Ang Zangbu Sherpa, a commercial jet airline pilot —just to name a few.

A modest and self-effacing man, Hillary has never drawn attention to his post-Everest accomplishments. Although he has written a number of books that describe his adventures and humanitarian work, he has avoided putting himself in the limelight. Thus Hillary's first response upon seeing the initial draft of this book was, "I am given much more credit than I deserve." It is my hope that *Sir Edmund Hillary & The People of Everest* will give the reader a glimpse into Sir Edmund Hillary's extraordinary life, while honoring and celebrating his remarkable achievements.

—*Anne Keiser*

(pg.10) KHUMBU HIMALAYAN PEAKS AT SUNRISE; *(right)* PHOTOGRAPHER, ANNE KEISER, CENTER, WITH LADY JUNE HILLARY AND SIR EDMUND HILLARY AT TENGBOCHE MONASTERY; MT. EVEREST IN BACKGROUND.

The Conquest

Six-thirty a.m. Roped up and carrying oxygen tanks on their backs, the two men were kicking steps in the soft snow that sloped up to the Southeast Ridge, a spine of rock and snow rising steeply from the wind-raked saddle called the South Col. The ridge crested at a secondary pinnacle called South Summit and then continued to the highest place on earth—the top of Mount Everest, nearly six miles up in the sky.

The last 400 feet to the South Summit broadened and rose up in what the New Zealander called "appalling steepness." With their first steps on the vertical pitch he realized they were on dangerous ground, for the snow was loose and unstable and refused to pack into place. Their ice axes sank into it without any support. Only a thin crust of frozen snow held the unstable slope together. In the lead, the New Zealander was forcing his way upward with deep steps, when suddenly an area of crust all around him broke off in large sections and slid back with him. He stopped, but the crust, gathering speed, slid out of sight. He forged on. Again and again the thin crust gave way, and he sank through it up to his knees in soft snow, sometimes sliding back. It was tiring, exasperating work—and exceedingly dangerous. At any moment the whole slope might avalanche. But he exhorted himself onward: "Ed, my boy, this is Everest; you've got to push it a bit harder!"

The unconquered summit of Everest was the beckoning dream of all mountaineers. A first ascent of the mighty peak would be a landmark in mountaineering and one of the greatest of all adventures. The New Zealander plowed on, cautiously zigzagging upward. When he stopped, he could look down at Tibet, 10,000 feet below. A mistake, a poor decision, would be the end.

The lanky, lantern-jawed, 33-year-old beekeeper turned to his climbing partner: "Do you think we should go on?"

Tenzing Norgay Sherpa, charming, unflappable, and an exceptional climber, was on his sixth Everest expedition. He had participated in his first expedition in 1935 as a 21-year-old high-altitude porter and had reached within 800 feet of the summit on a Swiss expedition in 1952. Tenzing also considered the conditions extremely dangerous. But being a perfect gentleman, he replied, "Just as you wish."

It was exactly the reply Edmund Hillary had expected. The words would not help him much; the decision, Hillary knew, would have to be his. But Tenzing would never let him down.

(pg.14) HILLARY AT BASE CAMP AFTER TRIUMPHANT ASCENT; (pg.15—crescent) MT. EVEREST; (left) SHERPAS CROSSING CREVASSE; (above) PORTERS CARRYING SUPPLIES ON 1953 EVEREST EXPEDITION.

"Do you think we should go on?" asked Hillary. "Just as you wish," replied Tenzing.

Making frequent changes of lead, they continued their painstaking, perilous ascent. Finally they reached snow that was firmer, and the ice ax shaft went solidly into the snow, providing a firm belay to arrest a fall. After all the uncertainty below, the greater security seemed to Hillary like a reprieve to a condemned man.

At 9:00 a.m. they reached their first goal—the South Summit. Above, the sky was a piercing cobalt blue, its stainless dome vaulting over a vast creation of one icy Himalayan peak after another. These are the world's highest mountains—Lhotse, Makalu, Cho Oyu, Kanchenjunga. Only the second highest mountain, K2 in the Karakorum Range, is not part of these mighty Himalayas. To the North, the arid Tibetan plateau stretched in a brown haze to the horizon. Ahead, the true summit soared up in a steep pinnacle of rock and ice.

The two men paused to remove their oxygen masks and change to a full cylinder of oxygen but then set off again quickly, for Hillary was impatient to resume the climb.

(top) MT. EVEREST AT LEFT AND NEIGHBORING PEAKS FROM SAGARMATHA NATIONAL PARK HEADQUARTERS; (above) TENZING NORGAY SHERPA AND HILLARY DRINKING TEA AT CAMP IV ON THEIR RETURN FROM THE SUMMIT (MAY 30TH); (right) MAP SHOWING ROUTE OF 1953 EXPEDITION LED BY COLONEL JOHN HUNT.

VIEW FROM WEST
Buildup Phase

Mount Everest 29,002 feet
*Five and one-half
miles high*

Northeast Ridge

Southeast Ridge

Lhotse 27,890 feet

CAMP VIII, 25,800 feet. Pitched
May 24 by Hunt, Bourdillon, and
Evans; 19 Sherpas reached here,
six of them twice, packing 500
pounds of supplies.

South
Face

South Col

THE TRAVERSE, first made by Noyce and Annullu, next
day Hillary, Tenzing, and Wylie led 14 Sherpas across

Geneva Spur

Lhotse Face

Nuptse
25,680
feet

CAMP VII, 24,000 feet. Halfway on grueling climb from
Camp V to South Col.

CAMP VI, 23,000 feet. Used brief-
ly during trailmaking on the lower
part of Lhotse Face.

Lhotse Glacier

Western Cwm

CAMP V, 22,000 feet.
Foot of Lhotse Face.

CAMP IV, Advance Base. Here at
21,200 feet as many as 30 men
lived in a tent village while supporting the assault parties.

Khumbu Glacier

Stifling heat in the morning,
snow every afternoon, and
night temperatures as low
as minus 14° F.

CAMP III, 20,200 feet, 100 less than
McKinley, North America's highest
peak, was the lower terminal for supplies being packed up the Western
Cwm.

Rope Ladder

Nutcracker

Pack trail located in
center of icefall to
avoid avalanches.

CAMP II, 19,400 feet. This rest station
for pack teams was abandoned because
of alarming glacial movements.

Atom-bomb
Area

Lho La (Pass)
½ mile

Hell-fire
Alley

Hillary's Horror

Mike's Horror

THE KHUMBU ICEFALL. Gigantic
blocks of ice gradually shift down-
ward, 2,000 feet per mile. Three
tons of supplies were carried over
it to Camp III.

Khumbu Glacier

BASE CAMP, 17,900 feet. Eleven tons
of supplies were carried 13 miles from
Thyangboche by 450 porters.

© National Geographic Society
Drawn by Irvin E. Alleman

"The crisp snow and the smooth, easy blows of the ice ax all combined to make me feel a greater sense of power than I had ever felt at great altitudes before." —Hillary

(left) SHERPA CROSSING CREVASSE USING ALU-
MINUM LADDER AS A BRIDGE; *(right)* HILLARY
CHECKING OXYGEN TANK ON TENZING NOR-
GAY'S MASK BEFORE DEPARTING FROM CAMP IV.

He was remarkably fit and enormously strong. In years to
come other mountaineers on Everest would refer to the effort of
every movement on the heights, where the thin air has a third of the
oxygen at sea level. But Hillary described the climb five miles above
sea level as exhilarating work as they moved along the summit crest.
"The crisp snow and the smooth, easy blows of the ice ax all combined to make me feel a greater sense of power than I had ever felt
at great altitudes before."

Just ahead, however, the route to the true peak rose up above
them along a steep knife ridge of snow overhung by huge ice cornices.
Off to either side were immense drops. On the left, rock bluffs fell
steeply away 8,000 feet to the snow-filled valley of the Western

Cwm in Nepal. On the right, wind-carved snow cornices, billowing like frozen waves, projected over the precipitous east face, "only waiting," thought Hillary, "for the careless foot of the mountaineer to break them off and crash 10,000 feet to the Kangshung Glacier in Tibet." Here no one could help being excruciatingly aware that the slightest slip could be fatal.

On and on they climbed for two hours, moving steadily on a catwalk of firm, hard snow between precipice and cornice. Hillary was in the lead, cutting some forty steps and then stopping to rest and to belay the rope while Tenzing came up after him.

They came to a forbidding wall of vertical rock forty feet high, which spanned the ridge from edge to edge. Studying the grim obstacle, Hillary found one possible route of ascent—a narrow crack where the ice was breaking away from the rock. After taking a few deep breaths, Hillary wedged into the fissure, clawing upward as he kicked backward with his cramponed boots against the snow walls of the cornice. At any moment the snow could crumble and fall from the mountain—taking him with it. But the snow held, and he wriggled and levered himself up until his hand reached over the ledge of the cliff to pull himself up. For a few moments he lay there, too exhausted to move, then he belayed the rope while Tenzing came up, collapsing on the rocks after the ten-minute struggle. Now known as the Hillary Step, the spot was the last barrier to the summit.

From the top of the cliff the ridge continued with cornices on the right and the drop-off on the left. Hillary resumed chipping steps across an endless series of hummocks, moving steadily but more slowly. As he cut around one hump, another would come into view. Although the slope grew gentler, his original zest was now gone. His back and arms were beginning to tire, and he began to wonder how long he could continue. As he wondered, in his exhaustion, if the summit would be a precarious spot, he saw the ridge ahead drop away in a great curve. There was nothing above it. Nothing!

(above) CHARLES EVANS, LEFT, AND TOM BOURDILLON SETTING OUT AHEAD OF HILLARY AND TENZING ON MAY 26TH WHERE THEY REACHED THE SOUTH SUMMIT; (right) PHOTOGRAPH BY HILLARY SHOWING VIEW OF FOOTPRINTED RIDGE NEAR SOUTH PEAK.

At 11:30 a.m. on May 29, 1953, Edmund Hillary and Tenzing Norgay stood where none had stood before—29,035 feet above the sea, on top of the world. They had reached the summit of Mount Everest.

In years to come, when others reached the summit, some cried like babies, their tears turning to ice; some fell round each other's neck, laughing and crying at the same time; some fell on their knees and prayed. A diffident, private man, Hillary's first sensation was relief "that the summit had been reached before our oxygen supplies had dropped to a critical level." Then, as he recalls in *High Adventure*, his own account of the climb, "I felt a quiet glow of satisfaction. . . . I could see Tenzing's grin of sheer delight. I held out my hand, and in silence we shook in good Anglo-Saxon fashion. But this was not enough for Tenzing, and impulsively he threw his arm around my shoulders and we thumped each other on the back in mutual congratulations."

Hillary's famous first words to his friend, George Lowe, who set out from the South Col camp to meet them on the way down with a mug of soup, were characteristically low-key and offhand. "Well, we knocked the bastard off."

"I felt a quiet glow of satisfaction. . . . I could see Tenzing's grin of sheer delight. I held out my hand, and in silence we shook in good Anglo-Saxon fashion. But this was not enough for Tenzing, and impulsively he threw his arm around my shoulders and we thumped each other on the back in mutual congratulations."
—Hillary

(top left) TENZING AND HILLARY AFTER REACHING THE SUMMIT OF MT. EVEREST; (left) EXPEDITION MEMBER GEORGE LOWE AS HE RADIOS TO BASE CAMP WHILE HILLARY LOOKS ON; (right) TENZING NORGAY POSING WITH FLAGS ON SUMMIT OF MT. EVEREST FOR PHOTOGRAPH TAKEN BY HILLARY.

ON THE KHUMBU ICEFALL IS AN EVER-SHIFTING LABYRINTH OF GAPING CREVASSES AND ICE TOWERS WHERE MASSES OF ICE CAN TOPPLE AT ANY TIME AND SNOW BRIDGES CAN COLLAPSE INTO HIDDEN CHASMS. AVALANCHES ROAR DOWN THE LHOTSE FACE LIKE SUBWAY TRAINS. FIERCE STORMS AND BRUTAL WINDS BLAST THE SUMMIT, WHICH REACHES INTO THE JET STREAM FOR MOST OF THE YEAR.

TWO CLIMBERS DWARFED ON THE COLOSSAL KHUMBU ICEFALL IN THE WESTERN CWM AT 19,800 FEET. (IT TOOK THE 1953 EXPEDITION OVER A WEEK TO CREATE A ROUTE THROUGH TREACHEROUS CREVASSES AND MOVING ICE BLOCKS.)

Ever since 1856, when the Indian Survey Office recorded a mountain 29,002 feet high in Nepal, this summit had been the supreme goal of climbers. The first attempt came in 1921; three years later, in 1924, George Leigh Mallory and Andrew Irvine launched their highly publicized assault. Others followed, but for thirty-two years the indomitable mountain, named for Sir George Everest, a Surveyor General of India, continued to defy the efforts of the best climbers in the world. In fact, by 1953 Everest had claimed at least sixteen lives, and many more would die in later expeditions. (By 2002 the toll had risen to 172.)

Tackling the mountain presents a daunting array of hazards. On the Khumbu Icefall, an ever-shifting labyrinth of gaping crevasses and ice towers, masses of ice can topple at any time and snow bridges can collapse into hidden chasms. Avalanches roar down the Lhotse Face like subway trains. Fierce storms and brutal winds blast the summit, which reaches into the jet stream for most of the year. A break occurs in May, when the approaching monsoon forces the jet stream north. The few weeks between the departure of the winds and the onset of the snow-laden monsoon storms offer a window for climbing. Another opportunity arises in the lull after the monsoon departs in September, and before the mighty jet stream winds return. But weather can turn evil even during the two brief climbing seasons, sweeping in storms that are all the more deadly because they come unexpectedly.

The fearful effects of high altitude in the dangerously thin air pose other dangers. At the summit, air contains just one third of the oxygen at sea level, causing insomnia, headache, sore throat, nausea, diarrhea, loss of appetite, and a debilitating shortness of breath. Heavy breathing, at four times the rate at sea level, and low humidity deplete the body of moisture, bringing on dehydration unless about a gallon of water a day is consumed. The gravest hazard is a syndrome known as acute mountain sickness—AMS. It is characterized by either pulmonary edema, in which the lungs swell with water, or cerebral edema, in which the brain does. These ill effects can usually be avoided by acclimatization. But in the so-called "death zone," altitudes above 25,000 feet, the oxygen-starved human physiology starts to collapse. The brain slows down, concentration and clear thinking decline, muscles deteriorate, and the lack of oxygen makes it difficult to generate body heat, so the climber becomes more vulnerable to frostbite and hypothermia. The best way to deal with AMS is to get down fast, because if you stay in the death zone long enough, you die. Supplemental oxygen helps, but its supply is always limited.

THE ICEFALL IS FROZEN, BUT IT IS NEVER STILL. IT CREAKS AND CRACKLES WITH CONSTANT MOVEMENT THAT CAN SPLIT THE SERACS AND TRIGGER ENORMOUS AVALANCHES. . . .HUNT ASSIGNED AN ADVANCE PARTY TO FORGE A ROUTE THROUGH THIS COLLAPSING ICE AND MAKE IT AS SAFE AS POSSIBLE FOR THE LADEN AND INEXPERT PORTERS. HE PUT HILLARY IN CHARGE.

The 1953 expedition, under the command of British Army Colonel John Hunt, had prepared for the landmark day with a long, carefully planned siege of the mountain. It began in early March as the thirteen members of the expedition and a small army of men set out from a little village near Kathmandu, Nepal, for the Tengboche Monastery, fifteen miles from Base Camp. A contingent of 450 low-altitude porters carried their sixty-pound loads 175 miles, as far as Tengboche, and departed. Thirty-six handpicked Sherpas stayed on for high-altitude work, which consisted of lifting loads of food, cooking fuel, and oxygen to stock an ever-higher series of eight camps above Base Camp, in preparation for the summit assault launched from Camp Nine.

The first obstacle was at 18,000 feet at the Khumbu Icefall, where grass and greenery end and the most dreadful difficulties begin. Until this point, the route up Everest's southwest flank poses no obstacles and requires no mountaineering skills. But at the icefall, the glacier plunges down 2,000 feet in a frozen cascade about a mile and a half long, and the ice breaks into a jumble of huge, wobbly blocks called seracs, some as large as a twelve-story office

(top left) COLONEL JOHN HUNT, LEADER OF THE 1953 EVEREST EXPEDITION; (above) HILLARY CLIMBING WITH OXYGEN MASK AND TANK; (right) CROSSING CREVASSE; (overleaf) MT. EVEREST MASSIF FROM TENGBOCHE MONASTERY.

building. As the glacier moves, it also fractures into innumerable crevasses—some gaping clefts, some concealed by snow bridges that collapse suddenly into yawning depths.

The icefall is frozen, but it is never still. It creaks and crackles with constant movement that can split the seracs and trigger enormous avalanches. The tottering, shattered terrain has claimed many lives and is considered the toughest and most dangerous section of the whole climb.

Hunt assigned an advance party to forge a route through this collapsing ice and make it as safe as possible for the laden and inexpert porters. He put Hillary in charge.

Wearing crampons with iron spikes clamped to the soles of their boots, Hillary and his team headed up the icefall, tackling the crevasses with "a cautious examination and then a wild leap, if it wasn't too wide." For the really big ones, there was an anxious search for a snow bridge solid enough to hold their weight. Sometimes the chasms were spanned with a pine pole plugged into the snow on either side or aluminum ladders in six-foot sections bolted together. Sometimes a detour was the only way.

Hillary embarked on what he called an orgy of ice cutting to deal with the tottering ice blocks. When the climbers couldn't squeeze between them or even under them, he hacked steps and fixed ropes up and over their icy sides. The more threatening, or precarious, pinnacles and overhangs of ice were chopped away before the handholds were set and the route flagged.

"*We could do nothing to improve the unstable nature of the country, but at least we could reduce the length of time it was necessary to be in the danger zone,*" Hillary recalled. "*Care and caution,*" he asserted, "*would never make it through the icefall. If we didn't attack it that way, someone else would.*"—Hillary

"We could do nothing to improve the unstable nature of the country, but at least we could reduce the length of time it was necessary to be in the danger zone," Hillary recalled.

Although he was far from happy about the route's constant danger, Hillary was convinced it was the only way. The alternative was to abandon the attack altogether—which was unthinkable. "Care and caution," he asserted, "would never make it through the icefall. If we didn't attack it that way, someone else would."

The icefall led directly to the Western Cwm (pronounced "coom"), an enclosed valley, or box canyon, with a gently sloping, snowy floor. Advanced Base Camp was established there at 21,200 feet. Looming at the head of the valley was the great, broad, frozen Lhotse Face. To prepare for the final assault, the team would have to climb 4,000 vertical feet on the steep Lhotse face and then traverse to the South Col, the high saddle between Lhotse and Everest. In the cwm, wildly fluctuating temperatures posed an additional problem. By late morning, the sun's rays bouncing off every snowy slope turned the cwm into an inferno. Just as suddenly, afternoon clouds brought a snowstorm, and visibility was diminished to practically nil. At night everything was frozen solid in the tents, so it was necessary to fire up a primus stove to melt ice and snow for liquid. Even pens were thawed for writing.

On a reconnaissance in the Cwm, Hillary was tied to one rope with Tenzing, and could watch his climbing partner in action for the first time. He was delighted to find a man prepared to go hard and fast. Tenzing was someone who could match his own energy and determination.

But wind, cold, and snow had stalled the effort to cut a safe route across the steep and icy Lhotse Face for twelve days. Hillary chafed at being held back, "saved" for the final assault while others were attempting to establish Camp Eight at the South Col. He waited like a tiger on a leash, arguing with Hunt to let him go up and "finish off the job." In *High Adventure* he recalls his grim mood: "If we don't crack the route to the South Col pretty soon, we might as well go home; we were all sitting down here doing nothing while the expedition was crashing in ruins around our ears."

Then, in an about-face, Hunt surprised Hillary by letting him and Tenzing help the Sherpas to the South Col. They set off quickly, Tenzing and Hillary kicking and cutting a route while the Sherpas, some crawling on their hands and knees, struggled to the South Col with their loads. After three weeks on the Lhotse Face, the attack was on.

There, at 25,850 feet, was the base from which to launch the strike for the summit. Hillary and Tenzing readied themselves for the ultimate adventure.

HILLARY CHAFED AT BEING HELD BACK, "SAVED" FOR THE FINAL ASSAULT WHILE OTHERS WERE ATTEMPTING TO ESTABLISH CAMP EIGHT AT THE SOUTH COL. HE WAITED LIKE A TIGER ON A LEASH, ARGUING WITH HUNT TO LET HIM GO UP AND "FINISH OFF THE JOB."....IN AN ABOUT-FACE, HUNT SURPRISED HILLARY BY LETTING HIM AND TENZING HELP THE SHERPAS TO THE SOUTH COL. THEY SET OFF QUICKLY, TENZING AND HILLARY KICKING AND CUTTING A ROUTE WHILE THE SHERPAS, SOME CRAWLING ON THEIR HANDS AND KNEES, STRUGGLED TO THE SOUTH COL WITH THEIR LOADS. AFTER THREE WEEKS ON THE LHOTSE FACE, THE ATTACK WAS ON.

(top) PORTRAIT OF THE 1953 MT. EVEREST EXPEDITION; (bottom) COVER OF *THE ILLUSTRATED LONDON NEWS* WITH NEWS OF HISTORIC EVEREST ASCENT.

THE ILLUSTRATED LONDON NEWS.

The World Copyright of all the Editorial Matter, both Illustrations and Letterpress, is strictly reserved in Great Britain, the British Dominions and Colonies, Europe, and the United States of America

SATURDAY, JUNE 27, 1953.

THE CONQUERORS OF EVEREST: E. P. HILLARY (LEFT) AND TENSING BHUTIA, THE FIRST MEN TO SET FOOT ON
THE SUMMIT OF THE WORLD'S HIGHEST MOUNTAIN.

On the night of June 1-2, the eve of the Coronation, *The Times* received from the British Mount Everest Expedition, 1953, the message that E. P. Hillary and the Sherpa Tensing Bhutia, had reached the summit of the mountain, 29,002 ft. high, on May 29. It was later announced that the time of their triumph was 11.30 a.m. and that they stayed on the summit for about fifteen minutes. The news was taken directly to H.M. the Queen and published on the morning of her Coronation—a "crowning homage" for the great day. The Queen sent an immediate message of congratulation; and on June 8 it was announced that she had approved the conferring of a K.B.E. on Mr. E. P. Hillary and a Knighthood on Colonel John Hunt, the leader of the expedition. At the same time it was stated that she desired also to honour Tensing Bhutia, but that, since he is not a British subject, the form of the award would require consultation. He is classed as a citizen by both Nepal and India. A George Medal was offered and it is understood that Nepal has agreed to this.

(Photograph and excerpts by arrangement with "The Times.")

In the aftermath, there were parties and more parties. Crowds cheered and audiences applauded. Hillary was knighted by Queen Elizabeth II and became officially Sir Edmund Hillary, KBE (Knight Commander of the British Empire). Characteristically, his first thought when he received this news in Nepal was he would not be able to walk down the main street in his hometown in dirty overalls and would have to get new trousers.

Indeed, Hillary was little changed by adulation, and in the assault on Everest there is more than a hint of the man who would move beyond stardom as an athlete to greater celebrity as a humanitarian. Hillary's greatest journey—his greatest achievement—would only begin after the summit, when he sought to reach out to the people living in the highlands that lead to the great mountain.

CHAPTER TWO

The Vanished Sherpa World: The Way It Was

In 1960, in the Himalayas in remote northeastern Nepal, village elder Konjo Chhumbi prepared for his journey to Europe and the United States by packing a sun-dried carcass of a sheep, a bag of wheat, and some bricks of Tibetan tea. Eventually, he was persuaded to leave these provisions behind, but he was determined to take his silver teacup, embroidered boots, an assortment of fur caps, and necklaces of turquoise and coral. His gifts for Queen Elizabeth included yak tails with silver handles, which made excellent fly swatters—useful items for the Sherpas who could imagine no inhabited place without flies.

Konjo Chhumbi, age forty-eight, had been selected to accompany a sacred relic from his village monastery being taken abroad for scientific appraisal. The treasure, a cone-shaped hide sparsely covered with coarse hair, was esteemed by the Sherpas as the scalp of a Yeti, the legendary Abominable Snowman of the high Himalayas. The subject of numerous stories and legends, the Yeti was usually described as half-human and half-ape, with an overpowering stench, feet that pointed backward, and a high-pitched cry.

Did such an unknown primate really inhabit the mountain wilds of the Kingdom of Nepal? The Himalayan Scientific and Mountaineering

UNTIL THE KINGDOM OF NEPAL OPENED ITS DOORS IN 1949, TIME HAD VIRTUALLY STOOD STILL FOR THE SHERPA VILLAGES, PRESERVING A MEDIEVAL SOCIETY IN WHICH MONKS HAD A MONOPOLY ON LEARNING AND A DEEPLY SPIRITUAL PEOPLE LIVED IN CLOSE CONTACT WITH THEIR GODS AND DEMONS.

Expedition 1960-61, led by Sir Edmund Hillary, had as one of its objectives "to establish or refute the existence of the elusive creature." But in 1960 the Sherpas themselves had no doubts. Just as surely as the glistening summits were the homes of the Sherpa gods and potatoes were a staple of the local diet, Yetis were an accepted fact of Sherpa life.

Desmond Doig, the expedition's official reporter, negotiated with the elders of Khumjung village for permission to take their cherished Yeti scalp abroad for analysis by Western scientists. The elders feared its absence would bring famine, epidemics of dysentery, and other disasters, but finally they relented as a special concession to their friend, Sir Edmund, "the Burrah Sahib." (*Sahib*, pronounced like the automobile "Saab," simply means "sir." *Burrah* means "big.") The Sherpas voted to release the relic for six weeks on condition that three Sherpas pledge their homes and property for its prompt return and that Konjo Chhumbi go along as its escort.

The mission catapulted this elder from a distant village, which only a few outsiders had ever visited, into an unfamiliar world. Until the Kingdom of Nepal opened its doors in 1949, time had

(pg. 34) EARLY MORNING MIST AND HOUSEHOLD SMOKE SHROUDING KHUMJUNG VILLAGE BENEATH HIMALAYAN PEAK OF AMA DABLAM; (pg. 35—crescent) FARMERS PLOWING TERRACED POTATO FIELD IN SOLU DISTRICT; (above) KHUNDE VILLAGE IN MORNING MIST WITH HIMALAYAN PEAKS RISING IN BACKGROUND; (above right) KONJO CHHUMBI SHERPA, KHUMJUNG VILLAGE ELDER; (bottom) SHERPA BOY WITH YOUNGER SIBLING.

virtually stood still for the Sherpa villages, preserving a medieval society in which monks had a monopoly on learning and a deeply spiritual people lived in close contact with their gods and demons.

In the book *High in the Thin Cold Air* Doig noted that in every car and airplane Konjo Chhumbi boarded, he fervently mumbled prayers "to appease the local deities." Alarmed by the flash and roar of subway trains, he declared them the creations of the gods of the underworld. He wondered why Western women smelled so good and how they balanced on their high heels. In London he assured the Queen's equerry that he was not too disappointed in failing to meet Her Majesty, "the headman of many villages."

"She and I have many thousands of lives yet to live," he explained. "In one of them we will certainly meet."

To the scholars in Paris who ruled the scalp a fake—concluding that it had been molded from the hide of a serow, a species of goat-antelope—Konjo Chhumbi blithely responded, "In Nepal we have neither giraffes nor kangaroos, so we do not believe in them. In France there are no Yetis, and so you don't believe in them. I appreciate your ignorance."

Dizzying change would come soon. But at the time of Konjo Chhumbi's trip to the West, and for centuries beforehand, the Sherpas in their mountain villages remained untouched by the gadgets, ideas, and values of the West. Nepal, a country the size of Georgia in the U.S., was officially closed to foreigners by government decree, and its forbidding geography reinforced the policy, keeping Nepal outside the world's mainstream and its Sherpa hinterland more so.

"In Nepal we have neither giraffes nor kangaroos, so we do not believe in them. In France there are no Yetis, and so you don't believe in them. I appreciate your ignorance."
—Konjo Chhumbi

(left) SHERPANI WORKING IN RECENTLY PLANTED POTATO FIELD; (above) BARE-FOOT SHERPANI CARRYING LOAD UP STEEP TRAIL; (right) PRAYER FLAGS WITH HIMALAYAN PEAKS RISING IN BACK-GROUND; (below) SHERPAS WITH LADEN YAK ON WAY TO NAMCHE BAZAR.

There is perhaps no more corrugated landscape on earth than the 180 miles between Kathmandu, which stands at an elevation of 4,200 feet, and Namche Bazar (usually called Namche), the more-than-two-mile-high commercial hub and administrative headquarters of Khumbu. The intervening miles cut across the Himalayan watershed, making the trail a roller coaster of abrupt rises and slithering descents into valleys drained by plunging rivers. Then, as now, no road traversed the length of this backcountry and Sherpa homeland. Its three parts consist of Khumbu, immediately south of Everest, near the Tibetan border, Pharak, farther south, and Solu. Loftiest of all are the valleys of Khumbu, home of the high-altitude porters whose names are part of the history of Himalayan climbing.

To mountaineers, Khumbu is a realm of glaciers, avalanches, and soaring peaks that challenge their skills and boldness. To the Sherpas, it is forests, potato fields, pasturelands where they raise yaks—and home.

Until 1964 the only way to reach Khumbu from Kathmandu was by sixteen days of hard walking on a meager footpath—hardly any of it over level ground. The path threads through high passes

with vistas of great white summits shining on the northern horizon; it zigzags through forests dense with rhododendron and pine; it plummets down to rushing glacier-fed torrents that rumble and foam through great gorges spanned only by logs or by swaying plank bridges no pack animal could cross. Eventually the steep hillsides terraced with rice fields give way to plots of barley and potatoes surrounded by low stone fences. When the rivers run wilder and the snow peaks loom closer, the trail has left the realm of Hindu Nepal and entered Buddhist Khumbu.

(top) THREE SHERPANIS WORKING IN POTATO FIELD; (right) TWO SHERPANIS IN COSTUMES FOR OSHO CEREMONY TO CELEBRATE NEWLY PLANTED POTATO FIELDS; (far right) STEEP RIVER VALLEY NEAR VILLAGE OF BUNG IN SOLO DISTRICT.

When the rivers run wilder and the snow peaks loom closer, the trail has left the realm of Hindu Nepal and entered Buddhist Khumbu.

The Sherpas are Mongoloid by race with slanting eyes and high cheekbones, and Tibetan by origin, migrating down from the north and first reaching this part of the Himalayas in the 16th century. Tibetan-Buddhist by faith, they revere the Dalai Lama, worry about their souls in the Tibetan-Buddhist fashion, and perform good deeds to earn merit for their next reincarnation. Their remarkable loyalty and cheerful good nature, so often exhibited in their work as high-altitude guides and porters, may well be an expression of their religious faith.

TIBETAN-BUDDHIST BY FAITH, THE SHERPAS REVERE THE DALAI LAMA, WORRY ABOUT THEIR SOULS IN THE TIBETAN-BUDDHIST FASHION, AND PERFORM GOOD DEEDS TO EARN MERIT FOR THEIR NEXT REINCARNATION.

Evidence of their Buddhist beliefs is visible everywhere. Prayer flags flutter before every dwelling and monastery, sending messages to the heavens. Dome-shaped monuments, called chortens, harbor sacred relics. Long, stone mani walls make their appearance in the middle of the trail. Made of big boulders and large slabs of rock, these prayer walls are usually chiseled with the Buddhist prayer, *Om Mane Padme Hum* repeated line after line. The frequently uttered mantra translated "Hail to the Jewel in the Lotus," invokes the Buddha, who is envisaged in the flower. Prayer wheels often carry the same mantra, and as a tap of the hand turns these large cylinders, each revolution conveys a prayer. Smaller prayer wheels are hand held and twirled, so as the worshipper is standing, sitting, or walking, endless supplications are sent to the gods.

(left) TWO LAMAS IN CEREMONIAL DRESS WITH LONG HORNS DURING MANI RIMDU CELEBRATION; (top) SHERPA IN CEREMONIAL LION MASK; (top right) SMILING SHERPANI; (bottom) CLOSE-UP OF MANI STONE WITH ENGRAVED PAINTED BUDDHIST PRAYER.

A Buddhist enclave in the Hindu Kingdom of Nepal, Khumbu was effectively isolated in the first half of the 20th century, its seclusion breached only by the Sherpas who migrated to find work in the British hill station of Darjeeling, India, just across Nepal's eastern border. During those years, many Darjeeling Sherpas served as high-altitude porters for the foreign expeditions to the Himalayan peaks and to the pioneering British explorations of Everest. In those days Nepal kept its borders closed, and climbers had to approach the mountain from Tibet. Without the Sherpas' strong, reliable assistance, the first ascents of the other big mountains—K2, Kangchenjunga, Nanga Parbat, Annapurna—would have been impossible.

During those expeditions the world began to learn of the Sherpas. Some earned the sobriquet "Tigers of the Snows," a title reserved for those who carried loads to 25,000 feet— higher than any other men in the world had done.

But Khumbu, little affected by influences from these Darjeeling Sherpas, remained in isolation, a realm in which disease was caused by evil spirits and

masked dancers masqueraded as gods to drive away demons. There were no motor vehicles, for roads did not exist, and in 1960 there were no printing presses, no public schools, no telephones, no electricity, no hospitals, and only one or two shops.

In the early 1960s the 3,000 or so Sherpas of Khumbu still lived much as their ancestors had when they first arrived from Tibet in the early 16th century. They grew their own food, wove their own cloth, and tended their herds of yaks and yak-cattle crossbreeds, moving up and down the mountain valleys according to their animals' grazing needs. Seasonal migration was a way of life, and in the search for summer pastures the Sherpas routinely went to over 15,000 feet.

The animals were beasts of burden that could carry well over one hundred pounds, and they provided food, clothing, even shelter.

"We ate mostly potatoes when I was a kid. We ate them boiled and dipped in salt, hot pepper, or yogurt ... fried, curried, mashed, served in stews, and formed into pancakes. ...We also fed them to livestock..."
—Ang Rita Sherpa

(left) BUDDIST CHORTEN WITH AMA DABLAM IN BACKGROUND; *(above)* BASKET OF POTATOES; *(right)* ANG DOOLI SHERPA COOKING POTATOES OVER WOODBURN-ING STOVE; *(below)* YAKS PASSING MANI WALL ON THE WAY TO NAMCHE BAZAR.

Yak hair was spun into wool and woven into cloth; the coarser hair was made into rope. The hides were tanned into leather, and yak milk provided yogurt, butter, and cheese. Once a year, in October, a family might butcher an animal. Freeze-dried and smoked, its meat would last through the cold until February or March.

"The meat had to stay in the family. As Buddhists, we could never kill animals as a business," explains Ang Rita Sherpa, one of the first college-educated Sherpas.

Introduction of the potato brought a significant change to Nepal in the middle of the 19th century. No one knows exactly where it came from, but it flourished in Khumbu's cold, small fields and produced a bigger harvest than the traditional barley. In a few years the Sherpas cultivated little else, and potatoes eventually ac-counted for 90 percent of all planted fields. In time the increased food supply triggered a population explosion.

"We ate mostly potatoes when I was a kid," says Ang Rita. "We ate them boiled and dipped in salt, hot pepper, or yogurt. We ate them fried, curried, mashed, served in stews, and formed into pancakes. We ate them at virtually every meal, and served them boiled as the most common snack. We also fed them to livestock, fermented and distilled them into *rakshi*, and dried and ground them into flour. Rice was used only on special occasions."

The two-story Sherpa houses of rough-cut, large stones were mortared with clay, yak dung, sand, and water. There was no glass for windows—only glazed paper for panes, and the lower level served as a barn for the family herd of yaks, naks (female yaks), and the more docile yak-cattle crossbreeds. The body heat of the animals stabled below added warmth to the living quarters.

The family lived upstairs, at the top of a dark, steep, rickety staircase, where life centered on the hearth with a crackling fire set in the one long, main room. Copper and brass pots, water containers, and bowls of chang, or beer, rested on wooden shelves around the walls of this room. For another popular beverage Himalayans

consider delicious, Sherpas mixed chunks of pressed Tibetan tea with hot water, salt, and yak butter in a churn. People sat on the floor or on low benches and carpets. In wealthier homes there was also a small chapel where butter lamps flickered before gilt statues of Buddha. The indoor toilet was a hole in a corner of the upper floor, with a pile of leaves placed below. Waste was regularly removed before the spring planting of potatoes and dug into the fields.

Hearths lacked chimneys, so smoke just drifted upward through the gloomy interiors, blackening everything above and collecting in little stalactites on the ceilings. Smoke seeping from every chink in the roof hovered in a cloud over all the buildings so that from the outside Sherpa houses looked like squat, fuming volcanoes.

The smoky houses brought on bronchitis and eye infections, but the more significant health problem was tuberculosis, made worse because Sherpas pass cups around from person to person. This killing disease affected the lungs, joints, spine, eyes, and skin of the victim.

Thirty-five years ago, smallpox was also a menace. "We didn't know how it was spread," says Sherpa doctor Mingma Gyelzen. He remembers how frightened people were when someone came down with the disease. "My parents told us to hide in the forest when a stranger approached our village."

"If anybody got sick, all he could do was go to a lama (a monk) or a shaman. Lamas prayed over the patient and sought to chase evil spirits away with incense and offerings of sacred juniper fire, while shamans beat their drums or sought a remedy by going into a trance."

Another treatment was drinking chang, the Sherpa beer made from potatoes or grain. Then, as now, the potent drink was also the mainstay of Sherpa hospitality.

Sherpas did not even have a midwife system. For help during childbirth they merely relied on a family member. On one of his early visits to Khumbu Hillary observed that the number of women who didn't survive childbirth was "appallingly high." Hillary also found that most of the Sherpa mothers with two or three children had actually borne four, five, or six, for a high percentage of children did not reach maturity.

But perhaps the greatest hazard the Sherpas faced was the extremity of their environment. Enduring a windswept landscape that was bitterly cold most of the year, covered with snow and ice, steep, rocky, and always perilous, it is not surprising that most of their injuries were dealt them by the harsh hand of Mother Nature. Fractures—not to mention fatalities—from slips and falls were commonplace.

ON ONE OF HIS EARLY VISITS
TO KHUMBU HILLARY OBSERVED
THAT THE NUMBER OF WOMEN
WHO DIDN'T SURVIVE CHILDBIRTH
WAS "APPALLINGLY HIGH." . . . .
MOST OF THE SHERPA MOTHERS
WITH TWO OR THREE CHILDREN
HAD ACTUALLY BORNE FOUR,
FIVE, OR SIX, FOR A HIGH
PERCENTAGE OF CHILDREN
DID NOT REACH MATURITY.

(top left) LONE SHERPANI NEAR MANI WALL;
(right) SHERPANI ELDER WITH TRADITIONAL
JEWELRY; *(left)* YOUNG HILL FEMALE PORTER
WITH TRADITIONAL "NAMASTE" GREETING.

Mountaineers were the first foreigners to walk the rough, rugged trail from Kathmandu, entering Khumbu for the first time in 1950. For the next fourteen years an increasing number of expeditions marched over the passes from Kathmandu as mountaineering grew as a sport. Then in 1964 the Sherpas under Hillary's direction leveled some potato fields to make a short, sloping airstrip at Lukla, a two-day walk from Namche. Hillary had been finding the sixteen-day march from Kathmandu with porter loads of equipment for his various projects time-consuming and tedious. The answer, he decided, was to build an airfield for STOL (short take off and landing) aircraft. The airstrip brought limited, fair-weather air service to Khumbu. But well into the '70s, nearly everything except potatoes and dried meat was still carried into Khumbu on porters' backs.

"There was no market in Khumbu in those days, so my older brothers and sisters spent much of their lives carrying supplies," says Ang Rita. "All merchandise—rice, maize, bags of cement, glass, nails, salt, kerosene, and eggs—came to Khumbu, hauled in wicker baskets slung on a porter's back and hung from a band across the

forehead. By the time people were forty, they had bald spots where the straps had worn away their hair."

Indeed, carrying loads had been a central feature of Sherpa life. Lhakpa Norbu Sherpa, like other youngsters his age, started transporting goods as a boy. Now age forty-five, and educated in New Zealand and the United States, he recalled his youth in Thami, a village on the way to the Tibetan Nangpa Pass. "In those days the value of a son was measured by how much he could carry." Lhakpa's father took trips into Tibet two or three times a year, trading Nepali iron, paper, and butter, mostly for salt and wool.

(above) SHERPANI CARRYING LOAD OF WOOD TO HER HOME;
(above right) VILLAGE AND FIELDS OF THAMI IN KHUMBU;
(right) LOAD-BEARING YAKS CROSSING DUDH KOSI RIVER ON SUSPENSION BRIDGE.

Although almost everybody owned a *zopkio* (a male cross-breed), used for plowing, it rarely served as a pack animal in this petty trade. "It wasn't practical to take pack animals down the valley in the old days because of rough and rugged trails and wobbly suspension bridges. One could easily lose expensive animals over the cliff into the river," Lhakpa explained. "It was easier for a man to 'chase' his wife and children down to the source of food in winter and to return in spring loaded with grains."

The hardiness and self-reliance of Sherpa women—Sherpanis—impressed the early mountaineer visitors to Khumbu. They found that the Sherpanis often did the same work as men, particularly when it came to carrying loads on trading journeys. Hillary once recalled hiring a very attractive young Sherpa girl to carry eighty pounds of potatoes during a 1951 Everest reconnaissance expedition.

"Immediately the whole atmosphere of the party lightened. All the young men were dashing about like young colts." However, Hillary noted with interest, "not one of them offered to carry part of her considerably heavier load."

Indeed, Sherpanis needed no such consideration. They were strong, accustomed to hard work. In farming, the men traditionally did the plowing, and the women the planting; the men the cross-breeding and the women the milking; but the roles were not firm. With the men gone for six months of the year on the hiking and climbing expeditions, the wives and children tended crops and minded the livestock for all of the spring and fall seasons. People did what needed to be done. This egalitarian attitude carries over into marriage, where the wife and husband are regarded as equal partners, with tolerance and mutual respect as a basis for the relationship.

But it was the Sherpa's loyalty, courage, and good humor in the face of adversity that made the greatest impression on the first Westerners in Khumbu. In 1953 Sherpa fortitude quickly won the admiration of expedition leader Sir John Hunt. In *Conquest of Everest*, he writes of a group of Sherpas, many of them women, who had plowed through heavy snow in felt boots, arriving in camp at the end of the day, cold and wet and "in wretched condition . . . with many cases of snow blindness. . . . But these Khumbu folk are tough and proud of it. All but a few, those worst affected by snow blindness, were cheerfully ready to start next morning . . . none the worse for their appalling hardships and making no complaints."

In the 1960-61 expedition led by Hillary, six Sherpas took turns carrying New Zealander Peter Mulgrew, who had suffered a stroke, down from the heights of Makalu, the world's fifth-highest peak. In his book *High in the Thin Cold Air*, Hillary writes that "this loyalty and keenness to help those stricken on a mountain are

(top left) SHERPANI; (above) YOUNG SHERPA BOY; (top middle) ANG DOOLI WITH "NAMASTE" GREETING; (far right) KHUMJUNG VILLAGE ELDER; (right) SHERPANI MOTHER AND YOUNG SON.

Perhaps it was said best by Kancha Sherpa, who carried oxygen canisters for Hillary and Tenzing: "Sherpa inside very good."

typical of the Sherpa people. Many a Sherpa has lost his life through remaining behind to help an injured climber."

One of those was the Sherpa Gaylay, who would not desert Willy Merkl, the leader of the 1934 German expedition on Nanga Parbat. Another was Pasang Kikuli, who climbed 7,000 feet from Base Camp to Camp Six on K2 in a single day and gave his life trying to rescue the ailing American Dudley Wolfe.

On the very first Everest attempt in 1921–22, six Sherpas climbed more than 2,400 feet from Camp Five to Camp Six to deliver a thermos of tea to sahibs after a storm. In 1963, on America's first Everest Expedition, two teams of four Sherpas carried two frostbitten victims on their backs in 400-yard relays. The Sherpas turned the 20-mile ordeal into a jovial rivalry.

In addition to their loyalty, strength, and fortitude, the Sherpas' unfailing good humor and personal warmth made them favorites of mountaineers. In fact, their disposition was considered one of their great charms.

"They pump your hand vigorously, beam with smiles, they are so glad to see you, that you feel you have known them all your life," recalled Frank Izzard, a British reporter who followed the 1953 British expedition as far as Base Camp.

In the first of his three books on the Sherpas, Austrian anthropologist Christoph von Furer-Haimendorf observed that it is not accidental that these people have become trusted guides and companions of innumerable foreign mountaineers. "The physical prowess of these sturdy mountain people is matched by that of other Bhotias (highlanders of Tibetan culture and language). . . but the Sherpas' moral fibre, reliability, and charm of manner are qualities one does not meet to the same degree among any of

the other Tibetan-speaking communities on Nepal's northern borders." Again, one might speculate that the Sherpas' spirituality, their Buddhist belief that good works in this life will effect a happier station in the next, is to some degree responsible for their remarkable nature.

But whatever the source, from his very first encounter with the Sherpas, Hillary was deeply touched by their loyalty, affection, and charm. He respected them for their remarkable toughness and courage. Perhaps admiration first began to evolve toward action in the spring of 1952, on the British Expedition to Cho Oyu. Hillary, his climbing partner, George Lowe, and a crew of three Sherpas had spent an arduous, harrowing day crossing a treacherous icefall, stumbling blindly through heavily falling snow from crevasse to crevasse. They could hear the dull boom of fresh snow avalanches but couldn't see anything. Finally, they reached the bottom of the icefall utterly exhausted.

(above) BUDDHIST LAMA AND YOUNG LAMA STUDENT AT KHUNDE MONASTERY; (right) SHERPANI SCHOOLGIRL WITH FLOWER LEI SHE HAS MADE FOR SIR EDUMUND HILLARY.

When they prepared to camp, the Sherpas wouldn't let Hillary and Lowe help. "Respectfully but firmly they sat us down while they pitched the tent," Hillary recollected. "They laid out our sleeping bags and put us in them. And before long they were thrusting hot mugs of delicious tea into our hands. We all sat around sipping and laughing like the bunch of old friends and comrades that we were."

That same night in 1952 Hillary said to George Lowe, "We've got to give something back to these chaps."

In his book, *Schoolhouse in the Clouds,* Hillary paid tribute to what he had gained over the years with the Sherpas, "not only in the physical sense—so many loads carried here, so many risks taken there, or so many lives (alas) lost somewhere else. But few of us had failed to learn something from the character and temperament of the men themselves—their hardiness and cheerfulness, their vigor and loyalty and their freedom from our civilized curse of self-pity."

Perhaps it was said best by Kancha Sherpa, a man who went from walking the trail to Tibet in grass-lined felt boots to climbing to the South Col with crampons and ice ax to carry oxygen canisters for Hillary and Tenzing: "Sherpa inside very good."

Admiring the Sherpas for their fine qualities and grateful for their loyal and courageous service, Hillary pledged to leave behind something more lasting than just a memory.

IN HIS BOOK, *SCHOOLHOUSE IN THE CLOUDS,* HILLARY PAID TRIBUTE TO WHAT HE HAD GAINED OVER THE YEARS WITH THE SHERPAS . . . " FEW OF US HAD FAILED TO LEARN SOMETHING FROM THE CHARACTER AND TEMPERAMENT OF THE MEN THEMSELVES—THEIR HARDINESS AND CHEERFULNESS, THEIR VIGOR AND LOYALTY AND THEIR FREEDOM FROM OUR CIVILIZED CURSE OF SELF-PITY."

CHAPTER THREE

Measure of the Man

Even at age eighty-three, Sir Edmund Percival Hillary, a tall, strapping man with craggy features, large, bushy eyebrows, and big, strong hands, strikes you as a man of rugged toughness. His long, deeply lined face possesses a rough-hewn severity you find in profiles on old Roman coins. In repose he can have a somewhat grumpy look that disappears when his face lights up with a warm smile. His unruly mane of silver hair and slightly rumpled aspect underscore his blunt, down-to-earth manner and contribute to a certain air of nonchalance—until his pale blue eyes narrow in appraisal. At all times, his presence is commanding. And to those who know Hillary, his determination is legendary.

Hillary was born July 20, 1919, in Tuakau, a little country township forty miles from Auckland, where, whether "wet, fine, or frosty," children walked barefooted to the primary school. Oddly, considering subsequent developments, young Ed never became involved in school sports or other activities because of his small size. Nor was he permitted to play games after school with classmates, for his mother deemed them unsuitable company. He spent much of his childhood reading adventure books and daydreaming of doing all sorts of heroic things. At times he played with his younger brother, Rex, or he would rush around the paddocks of the family farm by himself with a wooden sword and, as he describes it, "slash madly in every direction to rescue fair maidens being carried away by villains." But he preferred most of all to head off over the fields on long walks by himself. "Fifteen miles was nothing," he recalled.

With Rex and June, his older sister, Ed led a simple, provincial life on seven acres of land, where the family grew much of its own food, grazed half a dozen cows, and made honey from an increasing number of hives. Their father, Percy, a country newspaper editor, abandoned journalism after a falling out with his newspaper's directors and turned to his bee-keeping hobby for a living.

(pg.56) SIR EDMUND HILLARY IN 1985; *(pg.57–crescent)* SHERPANI GREETING HILLARY WITH *KATA* ON TRAIL IN KHUMBU; *(above)* HILLARY, RIGHT, WITH BROTHER REX AND SISTER JUNE; *(right)* HILLARY AT 20 MONTHS; *(below)* GRANDMOTHER HILLARY, WHO WAS AN INSPIRATION TO YOUNG EDMUND.

Strait-laced and Victorian, Percy set strict rules for his family. As Hillary recalls, "He tried to inflict very rigid views on us, and there were few aspects of our lives that escaped his critical supervision." For example, he believed that most human ailments were due to overeating, so his frequent remedy was "dieting," which Hillary remembers as a very trying experience for a young boy with a hearty appetite. "It did have an effect," he records. "I was most reluctant to acknowledge any illness unless I could hardly stand."

Despite Hillary's protests against his father's rules and restrictions—to say nothing of "many memorable confrontations in the wood shed"—he always maintained deep respect for his father and looked up to him as a man of courage and high principles.

"This was the period of the Depression, and I can remember my father becoming very indignant at the policy of burning food just to keep the price up," says Hillary. "He regarded that as an unjust, very horrible procedure and believed food should be given away instead to people who needed it."

Hillary also admired his father for being skilled with his hands. He built their home and had a knack for contriving things such as a bookrack to hang over the back of a cow, so he could read while he milked. However, as youngsters, both Edmund and June were often irked that their father's enthusiasm didn't always last to the end of a project and that their house never had all its rooms completed or properly furnished.

Perhaps reacting against this parental shortcoming, Hillary always took much pride in his perseverance. In a characteristically modest assessment of his abilities, Hillary says, "I had very ordinary talents. I wasn't by any means one of the hotshot intellectuals at school. I wasn't a great athlete at all, but despite all those ordinary sorts of things, I've always enjoyed a challenge, and once I make up my mind to do something, I am really quite good at going ahead and doing it. If I decided to undertake an expedition, I virtually nearly always carried it out."

Still, if you talk with Hillary for any length of time, you learn he admires both his parents as worthy people with traditional values.

"They felt it was the obligation of the Western countries to help the impoverished nations of the Third World, so I was raised with this strong sense of social responsibility for those fellow human beings who might be less fortunate," he says with pride. Time and again Hillary credits his parents for instilling in him the impulses that sustained his humanitarian efforts on behalf of the Sherpa people and that have set such an example of compassion before the world.

As Hillary explains it, "They had done so much for me and had so little. My family training simply swung into place. Instead of just idly talking about the Sherpas' problems, I decided I should jolly well do something about them."

(*below*) THE HILLARY FAMILY—REX, GERTRUDE, PERCY, JUNE AND EDMUND.

59

Hillary's mother, a former teacher, stressed the importance of a good education, and she spent a lot of time coaching her children at home. As a result, Hillary progressed rapidly through primary school, graduating at the age of eleven, two years younger than the average student.

Hillary describes himself at that age as "a restless, rather lonely child." Extremely intelligent but physically small, weak, and awkward, he was unaccustomed to mixing socially with anyone outside his own family. Nevertheless, after completing primary school, he was sent away to the prestigious Auckland Grammar. As a shy young boy from a rural background who spent four hours a day commuting to the big city school, he felt very much the outsider.

(left) HILLARY, LEFT, AND BROTHER REX MOVING BEE HIVES ON FAMILY BEE FARM; *(above)* HILLARY IN AIR FORCE UNIFORM WITH SISTER JUNE; *(right)* HILLARY IN 1950 DURING CLIMB IN NEW ZEALAND.

*"I developed
a deep feeling of
inferiority about my
physique. It wasn't
an inferiority about
what I could achieve,
but a solid convic-
tion about how
appalling I looked. . . .
I was the ninety-
seven-pound weak-
ling that needed Mr.
Atlas's help."*
—Hillary

This feeling was exacerbated the first weeks at the school, when young Ed's self-confidence received a blow he would never forget. As Hillary wrote in 1975, forty-five years later, "The gymnastics instructor cast his jaundiced eye over my scrawny physique, rolled his eyes to the heavens, and muttered, 'What will they send me next?' He told me my ribs flared out in a most unnatural fashion, my back needed straightening and my shoulders were rounded. He placed me in the misfit class."

"I developed a deep feeling of inferiority about my physique. It wasn't an inferiority about what I could achieve, but a solid conviction about how appalling I looked. . . . I was the ninety-seven-pound weakling that needed Mr. Atlas's help."

Hillary recalled the incident yet again in an interview with his biographer, Pat Booth, in the 1990s. His success on Everest, he asserted, "proved I wasn't such a loser as that fellow back at Grammar had suggested."

Hillary started to grow rapidly at age fourteen—five inches one year and four inches the next—until he reached his full height, an imposing six feet two. And while sports and social activities continued to elude him because of his long commute, he steadily gained strength and stamina. As he explains it, he was brought up to hard physical labor. He and his brother spent weekends and holidays helping with their father's beekeeping enterprise, and Hillary vividly remembers the heavy work moving the sixty-pound tins of honey and lugging boxes of honeycombs that could weigh ninety pounds each.

Every interesting life is said to have a defining moment. For Hillary, it came in 1935, when he was 16 years old and on a school excursion to Mount Ruapehu, about 230 miles south of Auckland. Even then he sensed something special had happened to him.

"We arrived at midnight after a heavy snowfall had covered all the trees. As our bus carried us up to the hotel, we entered a fairyland of glistening snow and frozen streams with the mountain all shining and white in the moonlight," he recalls. "I was strangely stirred by it all."

Hillary still remembers it as "the most exciting experience I had ever had. . . . It was here that I developed a taste for snow and the mountains that has never left me."

Compared to such exhilaration, Hillary looks back at his two years as a university student as a difficult time. "I lacked interest and concentration and didn't seem to be able to make any friends— or maybe I was too self-conscious to try hard. I filled my time with reading, dreaming, and long energetic walks." He saved tram fare by walking the five miles to the university and five miles back each day.

On Sundays he walked even more, seizing every opportunity to join other hikers in the nearby hills, and reveling in his own boundless energy. Then, at age twenty, Hillary suddenly found himself on his first climb. He made the spur-of-the-moment decision after encountering two famous mountaineers during a brief vacation in the Southern Alps. The pair, "fit and tanned," represented everything the gangly youth longed for, and Hillary was "filled with an immense sense of futility at the dull and mundane nature" of his own existence. Then and there he determined, "Tomorrow I must climb something!"

(left) HILLARY IN KHUMBU, 1983; (right) YOUNG HILLARY ON TOP OF NEW ZEALAND'S MT. SEALLY IN 1947.

Without experience or equipment, he hired a guide who led off at a pace that soon proved too slow and steady for Hillary's liking. After a while, unable to restrain himself any longer, he dashed ahead. Soon he had scaled his first mountain, the 7,500-foot Mt. Olivier. "Making it through the snow to the ridge, then along the ridge and up to the summit really captured me." Utterly euphoric, he would never forget the intense pleasure of that day.

(above) CLIMBING THE GRAND TRAVERSE TOWARDS THE SUMMIT OF MT. COOK IN NEW ZEALAND WITH FAMED NEW ZEALAND ICE CLIMBER, HARRY AYRES; *(right)* BRITISH EXPLORER ERIC SHIPTON AT MT. EVEREST BASE CAMP ON 1951 RECONNAISSANCE TRIP.

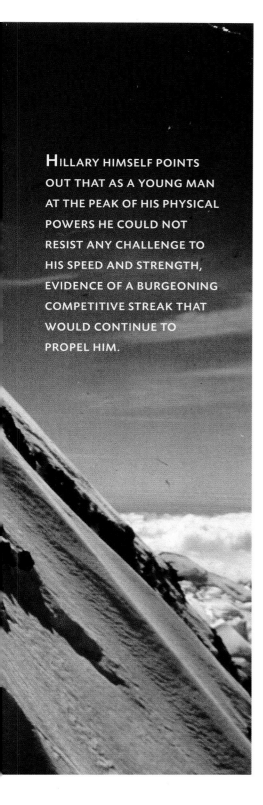

HILLARY HIMSELF POINTS OUT THAT AS A YOUNG MAN AT THE PEAK OF HIS PHYSICAL POWERS HE COULD NOT RESIST ANY CHALLENGE TO HIS SPEED AND STRENGTH, EVIDENCE OF A BURGEONING COMPETITIVE STREAK THAT WOULD CONTINUE TO PROPEL HIM.

At the outbreak of World War II in 1939, Hillary was working full time at beekeeping for his father. But at the beginning of 1944 he was called into the Royal New Zealand Air Force, which gave him more leisure time than farm life had. During his training as a navigator he gloried in the opportunity to cover some of New Zealand's challenging mountainous terrain.

He spent his tour of duty in Fiji and the Solomon Islands in the South Pacific as a navigator of Catalina flying boats on patrol, search, and mercy missions. While "most of the chaps spent their spare time lying panting on their beds," in the sweltering heat, he found much to do on his off-duty hours—sailing, crocodile hunting, and exploring nearby islands with a friend, a kindred spirit who was also "robust and restless." Hillary himself points out that as a young man at the peak of his physical powers he could not resist any challenge to his speed and strength, evidence of a burgeoning competitive streak that would continue to propel him.

His military career ended abruptly with a freak motorboat accident. He was hammering across a lagoon with a friend when the boat exploded into flames, blowing their clothes off. Burnt and naked, the two men, encouraging each other to go on, swam the two miles to shore. Because of the severity of his burns, Hillary's doctors predicted he would be hospitalized for many months, but he healed so rapidly that he was discharged in three weeks and was back climbing in New Zealand in less than two months.

From 1939 to 1946 Hillary had pursued his mountaineering in an offhand way. It wasn't until 1947, when he teamed up with Harry Ayres, an outstanding New Zealand climber, that he began a serious apprenticeship in snow and ice climbing and did some first ascents of snow and ice routes in the Southern Alps. However, Hillary is quick to point out that he was never a hotshot technical climber.

"I was strong, energetic, and had plenty of motivation," he says, "and I could always lug heavy loads around—often better than most. My greatest attributes were my enthusiasm and basic strength."

Then in 1951 Hillary was invited to join the distinguished British explorer Eric Shipton on the 1951 Everest reconnaissance. This historic expedition would be the first to discover the potential route

to the summit from the south, through the treacherous Khumbu Icefall up the Western Cwm to the South Col and along the Southeast Ridge.

His passage through the Khumbu District he would recall as the most exciting and dramatic three days he had ever spent. He wrote of "the rivers foaming through great gorges, the hillsides clothed in dense forest broken only here and there by a sheer rock face and the sharp crags. And then . . . towered the unbelievable peaks . . . mighty ice-fluted faces, terrific rock buttresses, and razor-sharp jagged ice ridges soaring up to impossible summits."

Physically he was in superb shape. He was tough mentally, too—with the guts and determination to triumph over his fears. But Hillary readily acknowledges being petrified a great deal of the time. In *Nothing Venture, Nothing Win* he writes, "In a sense fear became a friend . . . it added spice to the challenge and satisfaction to the conquest."

In fact, fear was a stimulant—an impetus to action for Hillary, allowing him to solve problems he might not otherwise solve. He often referred to "the pleasure of being scared to death, but persisting and carrying on nevertheless." If, as he believed, fear made you more alert and forced you to extend yourself, he must have felt a full charge of the emotion on that morning in 1953 as he and

"*. . .And then . . . towered the unbelievable peaks . . . mighty ice-fluted faces, terrific rock buttresses, and razor-sharp jagged ice ridges soaring up to impossible summits.*"—Hillary

(above) HILLARY DURING 1954 EXPEDITION TO MAKALU; *(right)* HIMALAYAN PEAK TAMSERKU NEAR KHUMJUNG VILLAGE.

Tenzing faced the ice-crusted, 40-foot vertical wall that loomed as the last barrier between them and the peak of Everest.

Those historic moments of May 29 must also have confirmed Hillary's conviction that fear builds and enhances comradeship. Facing danger with companions, says Hillary, hardens your resolve and inspires you to give it everything you've got.

It's interesting to note that in times of stress and danger Hillary took no comfort in religion. "If I'm in a difficult or dangerous situation," he says, "I feel it's up to me, not God, or anybody else, to get me out of it. I prefer to meet the challenges myself, without calling upon God for help."

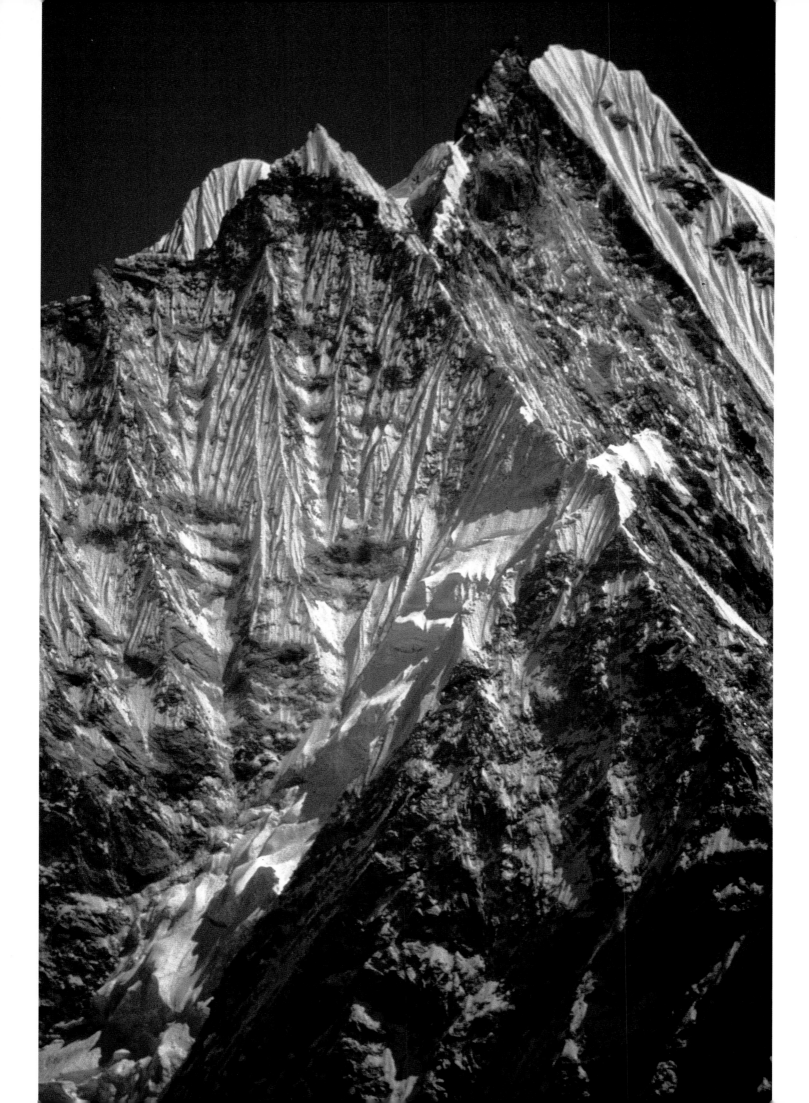

This attitude stands in fascinating contrast to that of the Sherpas—those very comrades with whom Hillary shared so much danger and whose strength, loyalty, and good cheer he found so remarkable. As his friend Peter Mulgrew once pointed out, there is nothing flamboyant about Hillary or his approach to mountaineering.

"Absolutely no showmanship." In his autobiography, Mulgrew paid tribute to his friend: ". . . at least on the surface, he is no text-book hero. Indeed, he can be scornful of the more romantic conceptions of mountaineering. All the same, it is probable that in their profound sincerity, his own conceptions of exploration and climbing mountains are the most romantic of all. To this man, adventure itself, and the ability of man by physical and moral training to conquer the erstwhile impossible are the basic ingredients of life."

In Hillary's scheme of things, persistence in the face of fear is what counts. By Hillary's definition an act becomes heroic only when it conquers fear. Difficult or dangerous deeds done in a casual way don't count. Hillary stepped onto the summit of Everest as a shy, socially awkward New Zealander. Very shortly thereafter he found himself on a lecture circuit in Europe and the United States.

His aversion to public speaking was another fear he successfully overcame, however, and from the moment Hillary entered the spotlight he began his transformation into a diplomat of poise and presence. He was still the unpretentious beekeeper who dreamed of adventure and dared to take risks, and yet he was never the same again. Sir Edmund Hillary, KBE, met with presidents and prime ministers, attended Buckingham Palace garden parties, and in seven days in New York was "forced to spend more on tips than I would have normally earned in a week at the bees."

(top) HILLARY AND FRIEND AND FELLOW CLIMBER GEORGE LOWE LEAVING AUCKLAND, N. Z. FOR KATHMANDU IN MARCH 1953 TO JOIN EVEREST EXPEDITION; (bottom) SIR EDMUND HILLARY, GEORGE LOWE, AND HILLARY'S MOTHER AFTER HE RECEIVED HIS KNIGHTHOOD IN LONDON.

NEW ZEALAND'S WEDDING OF THE YEAR: SIR EDMUND HILLARY AND HIS CHARMING BRIDE

The conqueror of Everest, Sir Edmund Hillary, and Lady Hillary (formerly Miss Louise Rose) smile happily as they leave the chapel of the Diocesan High School, Auckland, through an archway of ice-axes after their wedding last Thursday. They are attended by Miss Rosalie Goodyear, of Athenree, as bridesmaid, and Mr George Lowe, Sir Edmund's close friend and climbing companion, as best man. A "quiet" wedding had been planned; but 1500 people thronged the streets to acclaim the couple and to wish them well.

(top left) HILLARY AND LOUISE MARY ROSE ON WEDDING DAY, SEPTEMBER 1953; *(above)* HILLARY AND LOUISE WITH CHILDREN PETER, FAR LEFT, BELINDA, AND SARAH; *(left)* HILLARY AND LOUISE LEAVING CHURCH BENEATH ARCH OF CLIMBING PICKAXES. (AS PICTURED ON FRONT COVER OF *THE AUCKLAND WEEKLY NEWS*.)

Accompanying Hillary on this first of many lecture tours was his bride, Louise Mary Rose of Auckland, a vivacious, outgoing woman and talented musician who became the mother of his two daughters and son.

"Marrying Louise," he once wrote, "certainly proved the most sensible action I have ever taken." She was much more of an extrovert with a "bubbling enthusiasm and fresh open personality," which so many people found appealing. Early on he found that at official functions he could leave a great deal of the talking and entertaining to her while he "relaxed and admired." Perhaps more importantly, she "was kind enough to accept, and even encourage," his periodic restlessness and his lifelong battle against boredom and relentless quest for adventure.

ON AN EXPEDITION TO THE ANTARCTIC HILLARY AND HIS MEN
DROVE THEIR CONVOY OF TRACTORS WITH THEIR ELEVEN TONS OF
CARGO AROUND THE CLOCK . . . THE CONDITIONS COULD ONLY BE
CONSIDERED UGLY—WINDS GUSTING TO FIFTY KNOTS, TEMPERATURES
RUNNING BELOW -30°F, AND POOR VISIBILITY.

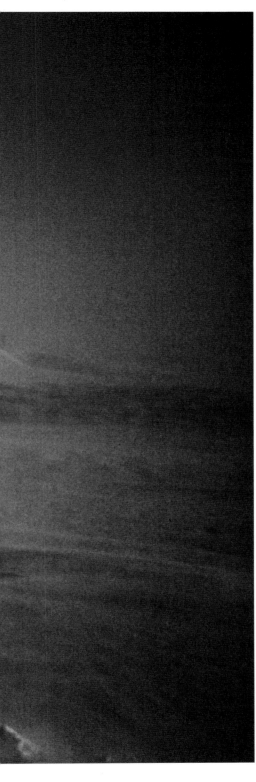

In the years after Everest, his wanderlust and relentless quest for adventure had taken the peripatetic Sir Edmund climbing in the Himalayas and on a lecture tour in Africa. Then, in 1958, he embarked on a major sixteen-month-long expedition to the South Pole. His mission in Antarctica was to provide logistic support for a crossing of the continent planned by British Dr. Vivian Fuchs.

It was not a perfect match. Hillary's flexible, pragmatic approach to any endeavor, along with his blunt, plainspoken manner, soon put him at odds with Fuchs, a more rigid, more autocratic man of considerable determination and toughness himself. Yet the two men had immense respect for one another and worked together amicably.

In a dazzling display of skill, daring, and sheer grit, Hillary and his men drove their convoy of tractors with their eleven tons of cargo around the clock, clanking their way across a terrain of deep snow and treacherous crevasses. The conditions could only be considered ugly—winds gusting to fifty knots, temperatures running below -30°F, and poor visibility.

Once he had established the supply depots, Hillary felt he had met his obligations to Fuchs and, thus, planned to use the "marvelous opportunity" to explore the "unvisited mountain country right at our doorstep." However, his plans to proceed on to the Pole were rejected by the committee administering New Zealand's participation in the project. Hillary then had no choice but to decide that field activities were his responsibility, and he continued on "as though the exchange of messages had never occurred."

"It was becoming clear to me that a supporting role was not my particular strength," observed Hillary in deft understatement. "Once we had done all that was asked of us and a good bit more, I could see no reason why we shouldn't organize a few interesting challenges for ourselves."

Although there was barely enough fuel for the 500-mile journey, Hillary determined to press on, a decision ballyhooed in the press as a race with Fuchs to the Pole. Hillary reached his goal with fuel left for only another twelve miles on January 4, 1958, sixteen days before Fuchs arrived on his traverse of the continent.

Hillary's account in his autobiography is typically low-key and candid: "We showed that if you were enthusiastic enough and had good mechanics, you could get a farm tractor to the South Pole—which doesn't sound much to risk your life for. The Press had a field day on the pros and cons of our journey, but for me the decision had been reasonably straightforward. I would have despised myself if I hadn't continued—it was as simple as that—I just had to go."

Hillary finds a wonderful analogy to the endeavor in Antarctica in today's space program, a highly regimented and technologically precise endeavor that would seem to have little room for men, like him, who are "not very good at taking orders." But perhaps some day, he hopes, "there'll be room in space for a different type of man—perhaps a little more like me—enthusiastic, resourceful, even a little irresponsible. They'll be found in all sorts of strange corners and they won't always have official permission. But when the pressure comes on, I'm inclined to think they'll perform, achieve, and die with the best there is."

(above) SNO-CAT STRADDLING CREVASSE; (below) MAKESHIFT HUT ON FROZEN ANTARCTIC LANDSCAPE; (right) SNO-CAT DRIVING ACROSS GLAZE OF ICE ON ANTARCTIC TERRAIN.

For about eighteen months Hillary returned to his work with the bees and a "more regular existence as a reliable family man." But the restless urge to get involved in another expedition surfaced by mid-1959, when the Field Enterprises Educational Corporation, publisher of *World Book Encyclopedia*, offered to finance Hillary's "dream expedition, a happy blend of science and mountaineering" in the Everest region. For eight months, beginning in September 1960, expedition members carried out research in such areas as Himalayan weather, plant and animal life, physiological effects of high-altitude endurance, and evidence of the existence of the Abominable Snowman. But as Hillary pointed out in a *New York Times* interview published some years later, "Science is used to raise money for the expeditions, but you really climb for the hell of it."

His team ascended 22,494-foot Ama Dablam and then made an oxygenless assault on mighty 27,824-foot Makalu. The mountaineers on the assault team were defeated a mere 370 feet from the summit. Other climbers suffered injuries and lung damage, while Hillary himself suffered a mild stroke.

That was to be Hillary's last serious climb, but when the expedition retreated from Makalu, he embarked on a different kind of endeavor. Hillary considers it as the most satisfying of his Himalayan adventures.

HILLARY AND OTHERS ASSEMBLING PREFABRICATED HUT ON 1960-61 SILVER HUT EXPEDITION. (THE EXPEDITION STUDIED THE EFFECTS OF HIGH ALTITUDE ON THE HUMAN BODY.)

"*Science is used to raise money for the expeditions, but you really climb for the hell of it.*"—Hillary

"In terms more meaningful than money," he explained, "we wanted to show our gratitude to the Sherpas—the high-altitude porters, cooks, and assistants from the village of Khumjung who had worked so hard for us in the mountains."

Hillary asked his Sherpa friends what he could do for them. The villagers responded with a unanimous request for a school. As one villager put it, "Our children have eyes, but still they cannot see."

So in 1961 Hillary built the first of the more than two dozen 'Hillary' schools in Sherpa-land and embarked on his lifelong commitment to the Sherpa community.

Fifty children, ranging in age from six to sixteen, attended those first classes, summoned to school by a school bell devised from an empty oxygen bottle. After the national anthem and prayer,

(far left) SHERPA SCHOOLBOY RINGING SCHOOL BELL MADE FROM AN EMPTY OXYGEN CYLINDER LEFT OVER FROM A CLIMBING EXPEDITION; *(middle)* HILLARY MEASURING DOORWAY OF NEW SCHOOL BUILDING; *(right)* YOUNG SCHOOL-GIRL WITH WOOD SLATE.

lessons were begun with emphasis on Nepali, the national language and the designated medium of instruction. The schoolmaster, a Sherpa imported from Darjeeling, began by calling out the letters of the Nepali alphabet and the Nepali words and sentences. The children repeated after him, shouting as loud as they could. The sounds reverberated against the tin roof and wafted out past the tall, white prayer flags fluttering before every house, past the stone-walled potato fields, to the stony ramparts of Khumbila, the sacred mountain that dominated the twin villages of Khumjung-Khunde at its base.

In the years that have followed, hundreds of petitions have been thrust into Hillary's hands during his annual trips to Sherpaland—to high-altitude Khumbu and Solu and its subregion of Pharak lying to the south. In response, Hillary, a private man at first uneasy with celebrity, took up a public career as a fundraiser and found the money to build twenty-six schools, two hospitals, a dozen medical clinics, numerous bridges and water systems, and an airstrip at Lukla, a two-day walk from Namche.

For himself, Sir Edmund has made a living as a consultant on camping and other outdoor equipment for Sears and as a director of the Australian subsidiary of the United States-based Field Enterprises Educational Corporation. But nothing has interfered with his ongoing effort on behalf of the Sherpa people.

Even when tragedy struck on March 31, 1975, when his wife Louise and one of his daughters, Belinda, were killed in a single-engine plane that crashed as it took off from Kathmandu, Hillary carried on. Over four decades his commitment has never wavered.

An earnest and deeply felt sense of justice and duty transformed Hillary, the conqueror of Everest, the somewhat reckless athlete, into a father figure and a humanitarian. With the Khumjung School, the first of Hillary's numerous projects, a new way of life was beginning for the Sherpas. For Hillary, with such exploits as scaling peaks and trekking across Antarctica long behind him, a greater adventure had begun.

AN EARNEST AND DEEPLY FELT SENSE OF JUSTICE AND DUTY TRANSFORMED HILLARY, THE CONQUEROR OF EVEREST, INTO A FATHER FIGURE AND A HUMANITARIAN . . . OVER FOUR DECADES HIS COMMITMENT HAS NEVER WAVERED.

(left) HILLARY SHARING A LIGHT MOMENT DURING A PETITION FROM SHERPAS TO HELP WITH A PROJECT; *(right)* A SATISFIED HILLARY ENJOYING A CELEBRATION AT KHUMJUNG SCHOOL IN 1990.

Hillary's One-Man Foreign-Aid Program

Not many pilots of jumbo jets have also worked as porters carrying sixty-pound loads for twelve rupees or twenty-five cents a day. But Ang Zangbu Sherpa has. The son of a potato farmer, he was a twelve-year-old student and working part-time as a porter to earn money for a small transistor radio.

"I wanted to improve my English by listening to the Voice of America and to learn what was going on in the rest of the world. I was the only student in the Khumjung school who owned a radio," recalled Captain Ang Zangbu Sherpa, a trim, boyishly handsome pilot with knowing eyes who has piloted passenger jets to Europe and China for Royal Nepal Airlines and now flies for Britannia Airways, based in Berlin, Germany.

Ang Zangbu began his studies when he turned six. There was no school in his village, so his father, a man determined to get his son some education, took him to live with relatives in Chaunrikharka, a hamlet that had one of the first Hillary-built-and-equipped schools.

After the second grade, illness interrupted the boy's education for two years. "But my parents encouraged me to return to school even though they thought there was little use in learning to deal with large numbers," he said. "They would ask me, 'Why do you bother learning such big sums? We are never going to get that much money.'"

To attend the third grade, ten-year-old Ang Zangbu transferred to another Hillary school in the village of Thami, where he had landed a job cooking and cleaning for the teacher in exchange for room and board. His chores included gathering firewood on weekends and fetching water every morning from a creek about a half-hour away.

"In those days we collected water in thirty-liter wooden casks, which were carried on our backs. These were heavy even when empty," he recalled. "The worst part was that the tops were wide open, so if you didn't walk in a perfectly balanced manner, the water would spill down your neck and back in icy trickles. As a result, I learned the exact location of every rock along my route."

For the fourth and fifth grades Ang Zangbu transferred to the Khumjung school, the first of the Hillary public schools and the top educational institution in Khumbu. The pupils learned mostly by rote, repeating aloud and committing to memory the words of the teacher. "If the students didn't call out the words properly, the teachers wielded a big stick. Those early teachers were strict but they were strong, good men," Ang Zangbu said.

Ang Zangbu was unable to get a job to cover living expenses while he attended the Khumjung school, so he had to live at home. That meant a five-hour walk each day. "I had to get up at six o'clock in the morning and start walking from an elevation of about 8,000 feet to Khumjung at over 12,400 feet. It took three hours up and two back down."

For a little extra income during his school years, he wove baskets, a skill he learned from his grandfather, and sold surplus food and gear discarded by trekkers and mountaineers at the end of their stay. "I got my first brand-new pair of corduroy trousers by selling trekkers' stuff," Ang Zangbu remembered.

As he grew older, he did all kinds of jobs on tourist treks during school holidays—working his way up from kitchen boy to cook to porter, and ultimately to the position of sirdar, or foreman, by the time he was eighteen years old.

"We didn't consider it a tough life because we didn't have anything to compare it with. We didn't know what the rest of the world was like. And in that lifestyle childhood is one long lesson that teaches you if you don't struggle, you don't survive."

Such was the Sherpa character: remarkable stamina, intense drive, innate cheerfulness, and totally devoid of what Hillary called "our civilized curse of self-pity." It's little wonder that these people won the stoic New Zealander's esteem and affection—along with his determination to repay the debt he felt he owed them.

To a considerable extent, Hillary attributed the Sherpas' sterling traits to their battle with their tough environment, and he declared that "the last thing I would wish to do is to remove them from the battle completely." But he saw a way to help: "Better to put some sharper weapons into Sherpa hands."

Foremost among these weapons was education. Writing on the subject in the '60s, he stated, "It would help Sherpas overcome the poverty, disease, and unnecessary discomforts present in every village. By learning to read and write in their own language, the Sherpas could take a more active interest in their national affairs, be more receptive to improvements in their agriculture, their homes, and their health."

No one could foresee the tremendous boom in commercial trekking that would bring visitors to Khumbu in such great numbers. Hillary, however, did predict that some people would want to come and see Mount Everest, and he realized that education would enable the Sherpas to take advantage of opportunities offered by this tourism.

Hillary had seen areas of the world where tourism had turned the local population into "downtrodden peons," with no means to control

(below) STUDENTS WALKING TO KHUMJUNG SCHOOL. (SOME CHILDREN WALK TWO TO THREE HOURS EACH WAY EVERY DAY TO ATTEND SCHOOL); (right) SHERPA SCHOOLGIRLS WITH TEXT BOOK.

or influence events in their homeland. People in the city took advantage of the changes and made all the money and decisions, to the detriment of their fellow citizens in rural areas. "I had no intention of letting that happen to my friends!" he declares.

Hillary was equally critical of "misdirected" programs in Third World countries that made the mistake of giving young people an education that had little application to their lives. He believed it resulted in "useless types who were too proud to use the strength of their hands if other work was not available." In fact, his initial plan was not to take the schools beyond the fifth or sixth grade. "Only those few pupils who made outstanding progress would be given more education with a view to filling the need for more teachers," he said.

Well aware of the double edge on the sword of progress, Hillary sometimes felt the Sherpas would live happier lives if they were left untouched, insulated by terrain from the outside world. But he realized that there was no chance of this. If changes were inevitable, Hillary believed he could introduce them with the sympathy and understanding that might mitigate the shock and pain of rapid development. "I could do it better than a lot of others would," he told his friend, George Lowe.

HILLARY PREDICTED PEOPLE WOULD COME TO SEE MOUNT EVEREST AND HE REALIZED THAT EDUCATION WOULD ENABLE THE SHERPAS TO TAKE ADVANTAGE OF OPPORTUNITIES OFFERED BY TOURISM.

Out of such convictions arose Hillary's one-man foreign-aid program, the guiding principle of which has always been to follow the wishes of the Sherpas themselves. These people had now become aware of such amenities as education, medical care, and a less arduous way of life, he observed, and they wanted these things for their children.

"I was doing what the Sherpas wanted us to do," Hillary declared, "be it building a school, a hospital, or a bridge—that was reason enough for me."

Hillary's policy has always been to wait for the initiative to come from the Sherpas themselves, from an individual community or group. And even then, the community's request for assistance must demonstrate a real need before Hillary will swing into action.

"I was doing what the Sherpas wanted us to do, be it building a school, a hospital, or a bridge—that was reason enough for me."
—Hillary

86

(left) HILLARY WORKING ON A DOORWAY AT BUNG MEDICAL CLINIC; (above) HILLARY AND TRUSTED SHERPA ASSISTANT MINGMA TSERING PAYING WORKERS UPON COMPLETION OF A BUILDING PROJECT.

"Sir Edmund's projects are planned jointly with the Sherpas, working with them in a personal, informal way," explains American Elizabeth Hawley, executive officer of the Himalayan Trust and a longtime resident of Nepal.

"Hillary goes into all the practical details to determine if the project is feasible. For example," she says, "he wants to know where they'd put the school? Who owns the land? Sixteen families. Well, do they agree to combine? Do they need to be compensated, or can they donate the land? What is the fair rate of compensation? How many children will come to the school?

"Then he asks for a commitment from the villagers themselves," Hawley continues. "He'll ask, 'If the Trust will pay for the building supplies, will the community pitch in with me and volunteer their labor?' He'll determine who will work on breaking rocks for the foundation, cut and trim the timber, and bring these materials to the site. The villages contribute the manual labor and supply the timber free. He'll pay for the skilled labor, teaching salaries, books, and supplies.

"He doesn't act as an all-knowing Great White Father who decides how things should be. It's only when the people come to him and press him for his help that he gets into it," says Hawley.

On occasion, though, Hillary has played a more paternal role—as when a Japanese-Nepalese company attempted to build an airstrip right through Khumjung's potato fields. As Hillary described it, the company was offering high prices, trying to persuade the villagers to sell their land. It was also promising to fly in food to compensate for the loss of potato production. Some of the Sherpas seemed tempted by these short-term benefits. Hillary was concerned about the long-term effect on the community and warned the people that if they made the sale, they would become "a dependent bunch of pensioners, lining up each week for handouts of food. What would happen to their pride and independence?" he asked them. Alerted to the consequences, not one villager sold his land.

"There is no question that Sir Ed is a father figure to the Sherpas, for we feel we could always go to him with our problems. We look up to him and feel enormous gratitude."
—Mingma Norbu

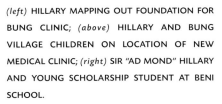

(left) HILLARY MAPPING OUT FOUNDATION FOR BUNG CLINIC; (above) HILLARY AND BUNG VILLAGE CHILDREN ON LOCATION OF NEW MEDICAL CLINIC; (right) SIR "AD MOND" HILLARY AND YOUNG SCHOLARSHIP STUDENT AT BENI SCHOOL.

"There is no question that Sir Ed is a father figure to the Sherpas," says Mingma Norbu Sherpa, one of the illustrious graduates of that first Khumjung class and now an executive with the World Wildlife Fund in Washington, D.C., "for we feel we could always go to him with our problems."

Mingma is quick to single out education as Hillary's greatest contribution: "Sir Ed's school program and his college scholarships to promising students have opened the door to new jobs and given Sherpas wider choices. With education, Sherpas don't have to labor only as porters or risk their lives as high-altitude climbers."

"Hillary's moral support has been equally important," adds Mingma. "He is always encouraging us to venture into new and different fields. We look up to him and feel enormous gratitude."

That gratitude is apparent in the excitement that spreads when Burrah Sahib enters a village on his annual visits. Hillary is feted and honored as something of a kindly deity; his arrival is heralded with the long, wavering notes of Tibetan trumpets. A procession of Sherpas greets him, bearing large bottles of rakshi, the local distilled liquor, and katas, which are placed around Hillary's neck. He is ushered through an archway festooned with garlands of rhododendron flowers to the village school, where, most fittingly, schoolchildren dance and sing in his honor.

THE KHUMJUNG SCHOOL, IN PARTICULAR, REMAINS A MECCA FOR
PEOPLE SEEKING AN EDUCATION IN THE AREA. AND THE HILLARY
SCHOOLS, IN GENERAL, ARE BETTER EQUIPPED WITH BOOKS
AND SUPPLIES FURNISHED BY THE HIMALAYAN TRUST.

(left) STUDENTS LINING UP IN THE MORNING FOR WARMUP EXERCISES AND SINGING NEPALI NATIONAL ANTHEM; (top) HILLARY AND HIS SON, PETER, ENJOYING A CELEBRATION AT KHUMJUNG SCHOOL IN 1983; (above)STUDENT AT KHUMJUNG SCHOOL.

The twenty-six schools in Solu-Khumbu, which Hillary helped build and equip, are now all part of the government school system, run by the ministry of education. By special agreement with the ministry, the Trust supplies books, teaching aids, scholarships, and funds for the maintenance of the buildings. Five of the Trust schools, including the one at Khumjung, have expanded to the secondary level, and the ones at Khumjung and Junbesi have hostels that provide lodging for students coming from more than a two-hour walk away.

The graduates of these Hillary high schools score very well on the national high-school graduation exam for the School Leaving Certificate (SLC), clearly a reflection of the Sherpa passion for learning and the quality of the education. One year, Ang Rita, a graduate of the first Khumjung class, topped the list for all Nepal.

The Khumjung school, in particular, remains a Mecca for people seeking an education in the area. And the Hillary schools, in general, are better equipped with books and supplies furnished by the Himalayan Trust. Needy children in the higher grades, whose families might not be able to spare them any longer from household responsibilities, receive small stipends, a fact which accounts for higher enrollment rates in the Hillary schools.

Education was not the only area of Sherpa life where Hillary discerned fundamental need. The utter dearth of modern medical services in Sherpa-land became vividly apparent to Hillary in 1963, when a deadly smallpox epidemic threatened the Sherpa population in Khumbu. Hillary and his nine-man team were on their way to Khumjung for a season of climbing and school-building when they came upon a distraught mother seeking help for her dying daughter. Every inch of the girl's body was covered with blisters and sores from the dread disease, which had been virtually wiped out in the rest of the world. As the Hillary team continued on to Namche, heading up the valley of the Dudh Kosi River, it encountered other cases and casualties. Because Sherpas were not vaccinated against smallpox, the disease was spreading, threatening to decimate the population.

When deputations from various villages came before Hillary, beseeching him to do what he could to stop the epidemic, Hillary

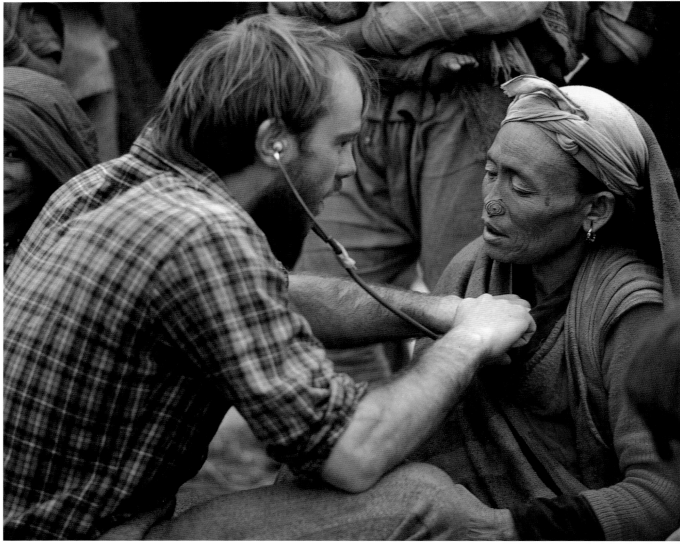

(top left) BUNG VILLAGER HAVING TEM-
PERATURE TAKEN AT IMPROVISED CLINIC;
(above) VILLAGERS WATCHING AS MED-
ICAL ASSISTANT UTTAR KABIR RAI TREATS
PATIENT; (right) UTTAR KABIR, WHO PETI-
TIONED HILLARY FOR BUNG CLINIC,
STANDING IN FRONT OF SHELVES FRESHLY
STOCKED WITH MEDICAL SUPPLIES; (left)
KHUNDE DOCTOR, KEITH BOSWELL, VISITS
BUNG TO INTRODUCE VILLAGERS TO
MEDICAL CARE.

mobilized his mountaineers into action. First he made a request over the government radio in Namche for an airdrop of small-pox vaccine from Kathmandu. Working with his team, which included two doctors, Hillary vaccinated several thousand people in a week in Solu-Khumbu.

Some thirty-five people died; others were left scarred and blinded, but a much greater disaster had been averted. A few weeks later, four village headmen of Khumjung went before Hillary with chang and white katas to express their thanks. "But for you we would all now be dead. You are undoubtedly the father and mother of our village," they proclaimed with deep feeling.

Indeed, when Hillary gives an account of his activities on behalf of the Sherpas, he cites building the hospital at Khunde as the fulfillment of one of his great ambitions. Until the construction of this facility in 1966, there was virtually no modern medical care in Khumbu. Almost 50 percent of the children died before the age of twenty—many of them from measles, respiratory infections, or dehydration as a result of diarrhea. Women frequently died in childbirth. There was a high incidence of tuberculosis, and lack of iodine in the diet caused a form of mental retardation known as cretinism. The deficiency also stunted growth and produced a disfiguring goiter, a swelling in the thyroid gland of the neck.

Hillary's war on disease in the region has produced dramatic results. The effort to combat iodine deficiency begun in 1966 with iodine injections has proven remarkably effective. Goiters have shrunk and cretinism has been reduced to almost zero in the new generation, automatically creating a community with a higher IQ.

"If you look at the statistics, even TB is way down," said Sally MacDonald, part of the Canadian husband-and-wife team of doctors at the

"Now the people still go to the lamas and shamans, but they will also come to the hospital."
—Kami Temba

WHEN HILLARY GIVES AN ACCOUNT OF HIS ACTIVITIES ON THE BEHALF OF THE SHERPAS, HE CITES BUILDING THE HOSPITAL AT KHUNDE AS THE FULFILLMENT OF ONE OF HIS GREAT AMBITIONS.

(top left) CANADIAN DOCTOR COUPLE WITH SHERPA PATIENT AT KHUNDE HOSPITAL; *(above)* KHUNDE HOSPITAL WITH SACRED MOUNT KUMBI-LA IN BACKGROUND; *(left)* HEALTH CLINIC ASSISTANT KAMI TEMBA SHERPA AT KHUNDE HOSPITAL IN 1990. (KAMI HAS RECENTLY RECEIVED HIS M.D. FROM THE UNIVERSITY OF FIJI ON A SCHOLARSHIP FROM THE SIR EDMUND HILLARY FOUNDATION IN CANADA. HE WILL BE NAMED CHIEF OF MEDICINE AT KHUNDE HOSPITAL IN 2002.)

Khunde Hospital in the mid '90s. Like all their predecessors, they were working as volunteers for a term of two years.

"Now the people still go to the lamas and shamans, but they will also come to the hospital," declares Kami Temba. "The lamas themselves encourage the people to resort to Western medicine." A compact, soft-spoken man with a gentle manner, Kami himself exemplifies the salutary influence of Hillary's dream. He resigned his position as health assistant at the Khunde Hospital in order to pursue his life's dream: he attended medical school in Fiji on a Himalayan Trust scholarship.

Raising money to build the Khunde Hospital dominated Hillary's life for a year in 1965. At first he tried to persuade the New Zealand government to support the project. When that failed, he decided to make a public appeal for funds, relying on a series of slide-show lectures—as many as five a day—to draw audiences. The campaign collected $30,000 for the construction of the hospital as well as for building materials, food, drugs, and equipment. Business organizations in New Zealand donated supplies, and assistance also came from Field Enterprises and Sears, American sponsors of Hillary's previous expeditions.

"I have been reluctant to appeal to corporations . . . you have to approach ten of them and be turned down nine times before you get the big bucks. And I never liked being turned down."
—Hillary

(above) HILLARY AND SHERPAS WORKING
TOGETHER AT BUNG CLINIC SITE; (right) UTTAR
KABIR RAI CARRYING BAG OF CEMENT AT BUNG
CLINIC SITE.

This work inaugurated a new aspect of Hillary's career, for ever
since then a significant portion of his time has been devoted to
fundraising lectures at Rotary Clubs, Lions Clubs, schools, and
black-tie dinners—not only in New Zealand but also in the United
States, Canada, Great Britain, and Germany.

"Most of the fundraising projects I'm involved in are relatively
small," says Hillary. "I have been reluctant to appeal to corporations. Generally, you have to approach ten of them and be turned
down nine times before you get the big bucks. And I never liked
being turned down," he adds with a sheepish smile.

"In my lectures, I just tell people a good story of my climb of Everest and show slides of projects under way. The people in the slides always look cheerful and attractive, and I gently suggest that a little bit of support would be very helpful," Hillary explains. "I consider fundraising the hardest thing I do, but I've found it quite worthwhile."

To administer the funds he had put aside for teachers' salaries and to maintain the Khumjung school building, Hillary set up the nonprofit Himalayan Trust in 1962. Later he established four subsidiary institutions, which exist solely for the purpose of raising funds for the Trust. In the United States the Hillary Foundation is based in Chicago; in Toronto, Canada, the Sir Edmund Hillary Foundation concentrates on supporting the Khunde Hospital and a reforestation program; the Sir Edmund Hillary Himalayan Trust is based in England; and the German organization in Bavaria devotes its funds to supporting the Hillary-built hospital at Phaplu in Solu, which has been taken over by the government.

The Himalayan Trust still actually runs the Khunde Hospital; however, in 1972 a signed agreement established a formal relationship between the Trust and the government of Nepal. Until that time, as Elizabeth Hawley puts it, Hillary had been operating "out of his hip pocket."

To ADMINISTER THE FUNDS HE HAD PUT ASIDE FOR TEACHERS' SALARIES AND TO MAINTAIN THE KHUMJUNG SCHOOL BUILDING, HILLARY SET UP THE NONPROFIT HIMALAYAN TRUST IN 1962. LATER HE ESTABLISHED FOUR SUBSIDIARY INSTITUTIONS, WHICH EXIST SOLELY FOR THE PURPOSE OF RAISING FUNDS FOR THE TRUST.

(top left) ANG RITA SHERPA, EXECUTIVE DIRECTOR OF HILLARY'S HIMALAYAN TRUST, AT TENGBOCHE MONASTERY SCHOOL SITE; *(top)* PORTER CARRYING ALUMINUM FOR A HILLARY PROJECT GREETING SIR EDMUND ON THE TRAIL; *(right)* LARRY WITHERBEE, PRESIDENT OF THE HILLARY FOUNDATION IN U.S., PAINT-ING WINDOW FRAMES FOR BUNG CLINIC; *(left)* HILLARY'S BROTHER, REX, A FRE-QUENT CARPENTER ON MANY OF THE BUILDING PROJECTS.

HILLARY HAS TACKLED THE PROBLEM OF DEFORESTATION IN KHUMBU. . . .IRONICALLY, HILLARY CONTRIBUTED TO THE PROBLEM BY CONSTRUCTING AN AIRSTRIP THAT HAS BROUGHT A FLOOD OF AIRBORNE VISITORS WITHIN TWO DAYS' WALK OF NAMCHE. CATERING TO THEIR DEMANDS FOR FIREWOOD HAS STRIPPED THE HILLSIDES OF THEIR FORESTS.

(above) TOURISTS AND SUPPLIES ARRIVING AT LUKLA AIRPORT BUILT BY HILLARY IN THE 1960S TO FACILITATE THE TRANSPORTING OF SUPPLIES FOR HIS BUILDING PROJECTS; (left) HILLSIDE AT PHARAK SHOWING THREAT OF EROSION DUE TO DEFORESTATION.

In 1977 at the end of his Ganges River expedition from the Bay of Bengal to the Himalayas, at 18,000 feet, Hillary developed a cerebral edema, a form of acute mountain sickness with a deadly buildup of fluid in the brain. Comatose and near death, he was dragged down to 15,500 feet encased in his sleeping bag and tent and then evacuated to a hospital on the plains of India. On his return to Khumbu the following year, he discovered each time he slept at over 14,000 feet he developed a severe headache. And he confessed he had lost some of his enjoyment of energetic walking.

Still, even at age eighty-three, Hillary's aid work in Nepal has not tapered off. In fact, it has found a new focus. While the main emphasis of his program has continued to be health and education, in more recent years Hillary has tackled the problem of deforestation in Khumbu. He considers the stripping of the mountainsides of their soil-holding forest cover a major problem. Too many trekkers and mountaineers came into the area too quickly. As a result, the great stands of conifers and the expanses of dark green juniper that greeted the early expeditions have seriously thinned and the slopes are exposed to erosion.

Ironically, Hillary contributed to the problem. In 1964, he had decided to construct an airstrip at the small village of Lukla to get twelve tons of building materials and supplies to his hospital site in Khunde. From Lukla everything would travel on the steep uphill trail to Khunde on the backs of Sherpa porters.

Hillary's motive was that the strip would cut about a week off of the trek from Kathmandu to Namche, which would be an immense boon to his projects. So, working for four weeks without the benefit of mechanized equipment, 110 Sherpa men and women hacked and shoveled out a STOL (short take off and landing) airstrip for small planes from a sloping patch of land. To compact the soil and level the field, he hosted a party, in effect, supplying a high-stepping crew of fifty Sherpas with enough chang to keep them dancing for two days, by which time they had stomped the strip smooth enough for planes to land. The pilots used the sloping surface to land uphill with the prevailing winds, so the upgrade would help the planes slow down.

With this landmark event Hillary had unwittingly forged a strategic link between Khumbu and the 20th century. The airfield, a tiny brown mark on the side of a mountain, also brought airborne visitors within two days' walk of Namche and, with them, enormous unforeseen consequences for the Sherpa villages. The easier access to the Khumbu gave a tremendous boost to the fledgling trekking industry.

The first trekking company was established in Kathmandu in 1964 by retired British army officer Colonel James (Jimmy) Roberts. He organized hiking tours with camping gear, kitchen staff, porters, guides, and supplies carried by hired help. Until then the trekking industry, now a popular form of adventure travel, had not existed anywhere. "How could anyone have any inkling in 1964," asks Elizabeth Hawley, "that the Lukla airstrip would funnel thousands of trekkers a year into Khumbu and change the Sherpa way of life forever?"

Hillary has written about being "racked by guilt" because the airfield was instrumental in unleashing the flood of trekkers into Khumbu. Catering to them, the Sherpas stripped the forests of firewood and the outsiders littered the hillsides with their trash.

"Lukla dynamited the dam that regulated the flow of tourists," says His Holiness, the abbot at the Tengboche Monastery, the spiritual center of Khumbu.

"The word Namche means 'dark.' When a place is dark, it means it is full of juniper trees," said an elderly Sherpa who remembers when thick forest blanketed the slopes above his village. Today little of these woodlands survive—only seedlings, and Namche's seventy two-story houses rise in tiers in an amphitheater of steep, barren ground.

(above) CLOSE-UP OF TREE STUMPS; (right) JUNIPER FORESTS IN MIST NEAR NAMCHE BAZAR; (below) NAMCHE BAZAR WITH ENCLOSED REFORESTATION PROJECT ABOVE THE VILLAGE.

"THE WORD NAMCHE MEANS 'DARK.' WHEN A PLACE IS DARK, IT MEANS IT IS FULL OF JUNIPER TREES," SAID AN ELDERLY SHERPA WHO REMEMBERS WHEN THICK FOREST BLANKETED THE SLOPES ABOVE HIS VILLAGE.

"The forests around Tengboche Monastery have lost their giant trees. And in the Khumbu Glacier Valley, you are lucky if you see a single juniper," mourns Hillary. He cites the denuded area near Everest Base Camp. "All the gnarled juniper trees have been cut. They ended up as great stacks of firewood for luxury fires for the climbers and hikers."

For centuries the Khumbu woodlands provided fuel for cooking and heating, and wood for building material for the 3,000 Sherpas living in Khumbu. Under traditional Sherpa law, only dead wood could be collected for fuel—a rule enforced by the village Forest Guardian, who also prevented overcutting. Simply calling public attention to the misdemeanor was considered punishment enough and was sufficient to deter most violations. But the ever-growing numbers of trekkers have brought a host of problems, the thorniest of which surrounds the demand for firewood. As anthropologist Fisher has pointed out, the astronomical sums the tourists were willing to pay for the pleasures of a big bonfire led to massive cutting. Even green wood was cut because it weighed more.

(left) EVIDENCE OF DEFORESTATION; (above) TREKKERS LINING THE TRAILS BETWEEN LUKLA AIRSTRIP AND NAMCHE BAZAR.

"In 1995 close to 15,000 tourists visited Khumbu. Each tourist brings an additional two people—porters or camp and kitchen personnel—making it another 30,000 people," declares Mingma Norbu Sherpa. "So we are talking about 45,000 people coming into a region with only 3,000 inhabitants and living there an average of ten days.

"During a single day, one trekker accompanied by his support staff can use up to ten times as much wood as a single Nepalese family. Many of them stop at tourist lodges and restaurants where meals are prepared for them on wood stoves. That has a big impact on a forest that grows slowly because of the high altitude."

As the demand for firewood and building timber escalated, the effect on the forest was devastating. By 1973 Hillary realized Khumbu's forests would disappear if some controls were not established on the cutting of firewood and building timber. He saw that and began working actively to organize a national park to place a protective mantle over the forests.

Hillary's efforts rallied support in Nepal and New Zealand and played a key role in the establishment of Sagarmatha National Park in 1976. (Sagarmatha, or Mother Goddess of the Mountain Snow, is what Nepalis call Everest.) At Hillary's urging, New Zealand and a number of world conservation organizations donated funds and staff for a park with headquarters on a hilltop above Namche. The 480-square-mile protected area contains three of the world's highest mountains—Everest, Lhotse, and Cho Oyu—as well as the Sherpa homeland.

The park's most important regulation is the ban on cutting green wood. Visitors are required by law to bring their own fuel—kerosene or gas. Sherpas may continue to collect firewood for their own use but may not sell it to tourists.

Created to protect what forest remains, the park was initially resisted by the Sherpas. They grumbled about the restrictions on grazing for their

yaks and their lack of access to firewood. Even Hillary was criticized for his support of the national park. His old friend, Konjo Chhumbi, rebuked him, saying, "Hillary first brought sugar to the lips of the Sherpas, but he is now throwing salt in their eyes."

But the park has gradually gained acceptance, and the people are now cooperating with its conservation program. Mountaineering and trekking groups are taking with them all the fuel they need. A series of small hydropower stations is bringing electricity to many villages in Khumbu, and increasingly the Sherpas are making greater use of electrical stoves for cooking and solar energy for heating water. In the meantime Hillary has initiated a reforestation program, and the Trust subsidizes the salary of workers who plant some 60,000 to 100,000 seedlings each year from two nurseries. The Trust also sponsors an annual visit from a forestry expert from New Zealand.

After establishing the Khumjung school, Hillary simply grew into the aid business. Of course, it was not conceived as a strategy or instrument of foreign policy, nor was it a work of pious charity. Reckon it as a labor of sheer friendship and affection for the Sherpa people. Perceive it embodied in the relationship between Hillary and his close friend, the late Mingma Tsering, who worked closely with Hillary on many of his building projects.

Mingma Tsering was a remarkable person who, though unable to read or write, had an amazing memory and was a natural leader of men. As Zeke O'Connor, president of Canada's Sir Edmund Hillary Foundation, explains it, "Mingma knew everybody's story and would know if what the Sherpas were asking for was really needed. Was a bridge really necessary or would a footpath do? At these village meetings Hillary relied on Mingma's judgment and assessment. An eye movement from Mingma would tell him what to do."

Mingma knew little English, and Hillary knew no Sherpa, but they communicated. Hillary explained it this way: "I understood Mingma perfectly well even though his English was rather complicated, and he, of course, understood me. Perhaps I can say I understood Mingma with my heart."

Indeed, Hillary's collaboration with the Sherpa people and his concern for the quality of their lives were driven by the promptings of his heart. As he has explained in his offhand way, "A certain amount of emotion comes into it. I got to know many of the Sherpas extremely well, and I have a great affection for these people."

Beneath Hillary's matter-of-fact façade lies the deep reservoir of compassion that inspired his good works in Nepal and took him from the summit of Everest to a much higher achievement.

In the final candid and thoughtful paragraphs of his memoir, published in 1976, Hillary writes that what really counts is not just

(above) THE LATE MINGMA TSERING SHERPA, HILLARY'S TRUSTED ASSISTANT WHO OVERSAW HIMALAYAN TRUST PROJECTS IN KHUMBU THROUGHOUT THE YEAR; (right) PORTRAIT OF A MOST SATISFIED HILLARY.

> *"Mingma knew everybody's story and would know if what the Sherpas were asking for was really needed. Was a bridge really necessary or would a footpath do? At these village meetings Hillary relied on Mingma's judgment and assessment. An eye movement from Mingma would tell him what to do."*
> —Zeke O'Connor

achieving things, "but the advantage you have taken of your opportunities and the opportunities you have created." He adds, "For me the most rewarding moments have not always been the great moments, for what can surpass a tear on your departure, joy on your return, or a trusting hand in yours."

Though Hillary was innately wary of expressing emotion, these poignant reflections provide insight into his compassionate nature. Hillary made himself famous by pitting his brain and brawn against nature, but it was the dictates of his heart that inspired and transformed the celebrity into an uncommon man.

CHAPTER FIVE

The Changing World of the Sherpas

In the old days, before the flood of tourists, Dingboche was a *yersa* village, a high-altitude summer settlement of stone huts with sod roofs. At its elevation of 14,500 feet, families would come here during the warmer months to pasture their herds and to grow potatoes and a little barley in the fields set between waist-high stone walls. But as visitors poured into Khumbu and Sherpas switched from herding yaks to herding trekkers, Dingboche became a stop on the trail to Everest. And the one-time forests of rhododendron, blue pine, and silver fir have now dwindled to a scattering of stunted junipers, giving Dingboche sweeping vistas of stupendous mountains, which erupt from the bleak, rolling tundra like thunder on a summer night.

When Hillary built his first school, Westerners came to this hinterland as climbers, not tourists. In 1964 a mere handful of twenty tourists made the trip to Khumbu. Eight years later the visitor count was over 2,200. Since then the number of visitors has grown phenomenally. By 1994 the Central Immigration Office, which issues permits for trekking, recorded the arrival of nearly 20,000 visitors to Khumbu during the year, a region where only 3,000 Sherpas live.

Fortuitously, the development of tourism coincided with the decline in the trans-Himalayan trade. When the Chinese occupation

of Tibet closed its Nepal border in 1959, traffic was stifled at most crossing points. Sherpas were beginning to feel the economic pinch. But as the trade with Tibet withered, mountaineering expeditions and tourist treks developed, offering unprecedented opportunities for employment and prosperity.

Sherpas, in fact, compare tourists to yaks. In the local idiom they say, "Like cattle, tourists give good milk, but only if they are well fed."

(pg. 110) SHERPANI ON CELL PHONE; (pg. 111–
crescent) SATELLITE DISH IN VILLAGE OF NAMCHE
BAZAR; (above) STUNTED TREES THAT REFLECT
CONCERNS OF REGROWTH AT HIGH ALTITUDE;
(right) TREKKERS DESCENDING TRAIL BUILT WITH
LOG SUPPORTS IN AN EFFORT TO HALT HILLSIDE
EROSION NEAR LUKLA.

Before James Fisher embarked on a career as an anthropologist, observing the sudden changes overtaking contemporary Sherpa villages, he was a member of the Hillary school-building expedition in 1964. Even then, as Hillary recalls, Jim was eager to understand how schools and tourism were affecting Sherpa society. Fisher returned to Nepal in 1974 and 1978 and again in 1986, and his book, *Sherpas, Reflections on Change in Himalayan Nepal*, chronicles the overwhelming impact of tourism on traditional life.

Tourism lured people of talent, education, and leadership away from farming and animal husbandry for six months of the year to new and better-paying jobs. Tourism also turned Sherpas away from teaching, with the result that Hillary's hopes for Sherpa schools staffed with Sherpa teachers have not materialized, and too few people were left full time in the villages to serve in the local councils or panchayats. Their absence has taken a toll on local political life. Lack of leadership has led to a fragmentation of village interests, says Fisher, "with different individuals or splinter groups promoting separate goals."

The labor shortage in agriculture has particularly affected the yersa lands. Since the spring and autumn trekking seasons coincide with the times for planting the harvest, Sherpa women have virtually taken over the job of cultivating potatoes and minding the livestock. Since the women cannot spend much time away from their main village, some of the yersa fields have been neglected or abandoned. Nevertheless, Sherpa farming continues to produce food for household consumption. New varieties of potatoes produce greater yields and have compensated for the decline of land under cultivation.

(top left) SHERPANI HARVESTING POTATOES NEAR
KHUMJUNG; (above) SHERPANI ELDERS INCLUD-
ING KHUMJUNG MAYOR, SEATED FAR LEFT; (left)
ANG PHURBA SHERPA, LODGE OWNER AND HEAD
OF SAGARMATHA POLLUTION AND CONSERVA-
TION CONTROL OUTSIDE HIS LODGE STORE.

Scarcity of able-bodied manpower has also curbed the
seasonal migration of herds to the yersa pastures. These days,
many Sherpas keep their livestock near their villages—even during
the growing season. As a result, quite a number of families have
switched to zhum for milk and to zopkio for transporting baggage,
for the yaks are only essential for the high altitudes—for carrying
gear for the fourteen or so expeditions each season at Everest Base
Camp and for supplying the small tent city there with fresh bread
and vegetables every few days.

In Dingboche, as in other yersas, the scattering of primitive
stone huts with low, sod roofs where the yak herders took shelter
have slumped with neglect or have been replaced by larger tourist
lodges. These rustic inns have been erected by Sherpas who have
retired from jobs in trekking and mountaineering—like Sona Hishi,
who started out as a high-altitude porter in climbing boots, crampons, goggles, and down expedition clothes. He soon exhibited his
skills as an organizer and manager and was promoted to sirdar, in
charge of recruiting and supervising teams of Sherpas, porters, and
support staff for major climbing expeditions. In the 1970s Hishi
was sirdar for the successful British attempt on the Southwest face
of Everest, for the Germans on Annapurna I and Annapurna II,
and for the Japanese on Dhaulagiri in Western Nepal.

"But after 1975," says Hishi, "my wife not agree for my climbing, because of the dangers. So I start doing trekking." The problem with trekking, he explained, was that the agencies in Kathmandu ended up with all the money. "Who sits at the table and has good idea with a good education, using telephone, and using head makes more money than who runs on the ground and works." Without an education, Hishi realized that operating a lodge offered a better opportunity than the trekking business.

Though his own generation missed out on the Hillary schools, Hishi is happy that his four sons have been more fortunate. Now the eldest is getting some experience in the trekking business as a guide. The second one is a monk, for Hishi has followed the Sherpa custom of dedicating the second-born son to the priesthood. The third helps him in the lodge and regularly goes down to Namche with a yak to buy provisions at the big Saturday market. The youngest son attends college in Kathmandu.

The problem with trekking, he explained, was that the agencies in Kathmandu ended up with all the money. "Who sits at the table and has good idea with a good education, using telephone, and using head makes more money than who runs on the ground and works."
—Sona Hishi

(top left) TREKKERS PAUSING FOR REFRESHMENTS AT A TEA SHOP ON TRAIL; *(right)* INCREASED TOURISM REFLECTED IN GROWTH OF TRAVEL OFFICES IN KATHMANDU IN 1999; *(left)* FEWER SIGNS IN 1983.

"*In the old days our hospitality was sincere. At that time the Sherpas had a very different image of Westerners. We used to think they were all strong men, wealthy and generous. Now so many foreigners have come, and we are so much exposed to the West, we know better.*"
—*Ang Rita Sherpa*

(left) ANG RITA SHERPA IN TRADITIONAL DRESS AND KATAS DELIVERING SPEECH AT TENGBOCHE MONASTERY IN KHUMBU; (top) NEW KHUMJUNG BAKERY THAT CATERS TO TOURIST DESIRES; (above) SHERPA DISPLAYING FRESHLY BAKED ROLLS AT KHUMJUNG BAKERY.

"I didn't have any yersa land, so this one land I bought it," Hishi said. "One American man from Los Angeles who trekked with me loaned me some money. I started with two rooms—a dining room and a kitchen. Then I made the sleeping rooms in a separate building so people would not be disturbed by noise."

That a one-time wage-earner could make such a business investment defines the new economy of the expedition era. Moreover, even for trekkers, wages don't represent the sole source of income. Tourism has presented a host of other opportunities for generating revenue. Some porters carry merchandise for a brisk trade on the side. Sirdars make extra money by employing their own pack animals on the trail, so most of them or their families have invested in zopkios. A few may also profit from overcharging tourists on the price of provisions and by reporting more porters than are actually employed.

Unfortunately, but predictably, the scrupulous honesty and unfailing loyalty that characterized Sherpa dealings with the mountaineers in early days have eroded. As Ang Rita Sherpa, the executive director of the Himalayan Trust, explained it, "In the old days our hospitality was sincere. At that time the Sherpas had a very different image of Westerners. We used to think they were all

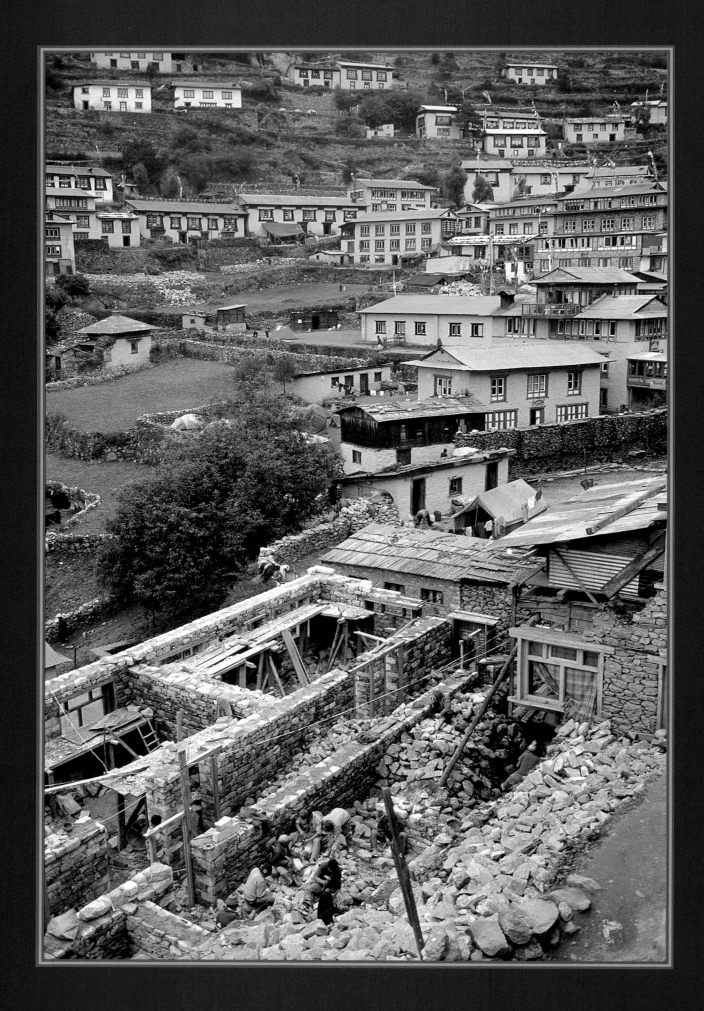

(left) SHERPAS INVESTING THEIR WEALTH IN CONSTRUCTION OF NEW LODGES FOR TOURISTS; (top) YAKS AND TOURISTS SHARING STORE-LINED STREETS OF NAMCHE BAZAR; (above) YAK BELLS ON DECORATED COLLARS ARE SOLD TO TOURISTS.

strong men, wealthy and generous. Now so many foreigners have come, and we are so much exposed to the West, we know better."

Hishi started as a porter earning a dollar a day. But as he points out, even at that rate porters were making as much as seven times the daily wage of field workers. The high-altitude porters were even better paid. The downside, he says, is having to pay tourist prices for rice and sugar. "All food is more expensive. Also many people have changed their diet, eating more dal bhat (lentils and rice) and vegetables. The tongue gets used to all the new food." For Hishi, the packed dining room and his lodge are a source of prosperity. At the long tables conversation gave way to the sounds of hungry people eating great quantities of food. At mid-afternoon most hikers had completed the day's walk, and the room filled with people traveling from lodge to lodge on their own—a practice referred to as teahouse trekking.

In fact, the number of visitors classified as independent travelers, the teahouse trekkers, has been steadily increasing in the last few years. For example, in Namche, a village of some 200 houses, every corner seems to hold a guest lodge, and construction projects are everywhere in evidence. The village streets resound with the clink of hammers breaking stone—and outdoor Muzak proclaiming a new prosperity.

(above) SHERPA BOY DRINKING SOFT DRINK. (SODAS ARE VERY EXPENSIVE IN KHUMBU AND CAUSE PREVIOUSLY UNKNOWN CAVITIES); (top right) ELECTRICITY BRINGING LIGHT TO NAMCHE BAZAR AT NIGHT. (IT ALSO BRINGS TELEVISION AND COMPUTERS); (right) DENTAL CLINIC AT NAMCHE BAZAR HELPING DEAL WITH DENTAL PROBLEMS AND ENCOURAGING DENTAL HYGIENE.

Sherpas have money as never before. They spend
it on jewelry, watches, radios, sleek sweaters, down parkas, alcohol,
and parties—and, now that electricity has come to many Khumbu
villages, the big item is television. Upgrading the houses with glass
windows and galvanized iron roofs was top priority several years
ago. Hand-split shingles and paper windows have all but disap-
peared. People who return to visit Namche after ten years are
thunderstruck by the changes.

The quest for the tourist rupee is shared by the lowland porters with wicker baskets on their backs; by the Tibetan street vendors, who spread their bowls of embroideries, beads, rings, spinning prayer wheels, and collapsible Tibetan trumpets on Namche's steep, narrow, crooked lanes; by the shopkeepers, who sell batteries, Band-Aids, and Mars bars and rent, buy, and sell mountain equipment; and by the proprietors of the bakeries, cafes, and rooftop restaurants who concoct milkshakes, cappuccinos, and egg drop soups in innovative ways.

There are more than 150 trekking companies in Kathmandu, some well-established and some fly-by-night and run on a shoe-string. Dozens of others have gone bankrupt. The larger organizations

THE QUEST FOR THE TOURIST
RUPEE IS SHARED BY THE LOW-
LAND PORTERS, THE TIBETAN
STREET VENDORS, THE SHOPKEEP-
ERS, AND THE PROPRIETORS
OF THE BAKERIES, CAFES, AND
ROOFTOP RESTAURANTS . . .

(top left) TIBETAN TRADER SPORTING A TOOTH-
LESS GRIN; (above) GOD-MASKED DOLL PUPPET
CAN BE TOURIST ITEM; (right) TIBETAN TRADER
SELLING TRINKETS ALONG THE TRAIL; (left)
GROUP OF PORTERS CARRYING MASSIVE PIECE OF
PIPE UP NAMCHE HILL.

have overseas agents and make all the arrangements for organized
trips and also provide guides and porters for independent travelers.
Sherpas now own more than three quarters of these enterprises
large and small.

Sherpas also own and operate lodges and shops, as well as
trekking agencies. They have developed additional business interests
in Kathmandu. And they continue to work as guides, cooks, and
camp staff on organized treks and serve as guides for many of the
independent travelers.

But not everyone is reveling in the new prosperity. Forty-two-year-old forester Lhakpa Norbu Sherpa, for one, worries about the over-dependence on tourism. "We are neglecting other opportunities," Lhakpa declares. "When someone has extra cash there is no place else to put it except into a house or a lodge. It's the one known method of investment. We need someone to show the way for cottage industries."

Lhakpa has a piercing intelligence and a straightforward manner that doesn't shy away from controversy. He is quick to raise his concerns that Namche has been overrun by the tourist trade. "There are hot showers and sewage that go with lodges. These strain Namche's limited water supply and waste-disposal systems," he says. "Even prosperous Namche has just the same two springs where people go to collect water."

A former Fulbright scholar with a master of science degree in forestry from the University of Washington in Seattle, Lhakpa

"Many of us are beginning to realize trekking is actually beginning to hinder the progress of the Sherpa people, luring away virtually every young man with leadership qualities for much of the year. It is hard to get any Sherpas to work for the park or teach school or to seek a political career. As a result we no longer have role models like the first Sherpa teachers at the Khumjung school who inspired the students."—Lhakpa Norbu Sherpa

(top left) LHAKPA NORBU SHERPA (left) REVIEWS FORESTRY PLAN WITH, LEFT TO RIGHT—GEORGE LOWE, ZEKE O'CONNOR, AND HILLARY; (inset) LHAKPA NORBU SHERPA; (top) LHAKPA RECEIVING AWARD AT MOUNTAIN SPIRIT AS THE FIRST SHERPA TO RECEIVE A PH.D.; (above) PORTERS CARRYING GRASS FODDER DOWN MOUNTAIN TRAIL FOR THEIR YAKS.

returned to the United States to do research and write his Ph.D. dissertation on the high-altitude forest. He studied the impact of the human factor—cutting, logging, firewood collection—on the forest structure in the Thami Valley. He is currently working for the Mountain Institute of West Virginia in Tibet.

Speaking in a lodge in Lower Thami, Lhakpa succinctly explains his deep interest in forestry: "I saw the need to reconcile the people's need for firewood, timber, and grass fodder for their animals with the need to protect the forest and its wildlife. With the heavy local demand for its resources, we can't simply protect the forest and let nature take its course. We have to manage the forest."

Lhakpa is also concerned that the good wages in the trekking industry are luring too many young men away from school after getting only basic academic skills. "Trekking provides an immediate good return with no commitments or investment of time that is hard to resist," he says. "You go up there, you make your money, and you come back. But you are not getting anywhere. Even if you climb Everest nine times, you are still climbing Everest.

"Many of us are beginning to realize trekking is actually beginning to hinder the progress of the Sherpa people, luring away virtually every young man with leadership qualities for much of the year. It is hard to get any Sherpas to work for the park or teach school or to seek a political career. As a result we no longer have role models like the first Sherpa teachers at the Khumjung school who inspired the students.

"In today's labor market," observes Lhakpa, "any young Sherpa who wants a job can get one. All he does to get on an expedition is to contact a sirdar, and if he is nice enough, he's hired."

From personal experience, Lhakpa also deplores the fact that the high-altitude Sherpas are not routinely trained in climbing techniques. "Last year a cousin of mine died on Everest. This guy was hired as a cook at Base Camp. With no climbing experience and no formal training in climbing techniques, he was allowed to work on the upper mountain as a climbing Sherpa. He died at Camp Three— fell off the slope. That should not be happening.

"The foreign climbers have a lot of money," says Lhakpa, "and they create incentives. We are still a poor people, so we are easily tempted to take something on even if we are not trained or qualified."

(top left) YOUNG SHERPA AS A BUSBOY, COOK'S ASSISTANT; (top right) DISMANTLING A CAMPSITE NEAR THAMO, VILLAGE IN BACKGROUND; (above) PORTER CARRYING ALUMINUM CHAIR FOR USE AT CAMPSITE; (left) TEA BROUGHT TO TENTS AS WAKE-UP CALL.

And yet, for Sherpas who lacked Lhakpa's educational opportunities, climbing has meant a livelihood. Among these is Ang Rita, who has topped Everest ten times—an individual record that stands today. Like Lhakpa, Ang Rita comes from a family of Thami potato farmers. But born in 1947, he is of the generation too old for the Hillary schools. Ang Rita knows, of course, that climbing is dangerous, but as he explained in an interview recorded in *Everest*, a collection of writings about the mountain edited by Peter Gilman, "Farming wasn't enough to support our family. . . . Since I had no education, I could find no other work."

With each successful ascent, reaching the summit became more and more important to Ang Rita. "Perhaps here was a path to success where I didn't need an education after all," he said. "Expeditions started asking for me. Now I have the experience many other sirdars and climbing Sherpas don't have. Many people die because their sirdars don't know the weather. They don't know the mountain."

"Overall," Ang Rita maintained, "mountaineering has been good to me and I think for most of the Sherpas. It has given us jobs and the chance to meet new people."

As Hillary foresaw, and as Lhakpa would certainly agree, education remains the key: "If young people learn to read and write," Ang Rita reflected, "they can choose what to do with their lives. I must keep climbing—I have no choice."

Today Ang Tsering's investment portfolio symbolizes the new economy. It includes not only Asian Trekking, which handles some twenty-five major mountaineering expeditions a year, but also Asian Airlines, the first company to use helicopters on regularly scheduled flights into the Khumbu.

(left) SUPPLIES BEING CARRIED IN KATHMANDU IN SAME STYLE AS IN KHUMBU; (above) TOURISTS GATHERING AT LUKLA FOR FLIGHTS TO KATHMANDU. (ONCE THREE OR FOUR FLIGHTS A DAY WENT BETWEEN THE TWO AIRSTRIPS; NOW THERE CAN BE MORE THAN TWENTY.)

Of those who have climbed aboard the tourist gravy train, Ang Tsering of Khumjung stands among the most successful. One of Khumbu's "Kathmandu millionaires," he is the son of Konjo Chhumbi, the Khumjung elder who accompanied Hillary and the yeti scalp to the United States and Europe in 1960.

Ang Tsering was almost eight years old and already taking yaks up to pasture when he enrolled in the Khumjung school. He went on to high school, to university in Kathmandu, and to medical school in India. But he abandoned his studies in favor of trekking. Lhakpa points out that had Ang Tsering been successful in getting a medical degree, he would have had to struggle for a while to make a living working in some remote, understaffed, undersupplied hospital. "Trekking made Ang Tsering a millionaire in no time," says Lhakpa.

Today Ang Tsering's investment portfolio symbolizes the new economy. It includes not only Asian Trekking, which handles some twenty-five major mountaineering expeditions a year, but also Asian Airlines, the first company to use helicopters on regularly scheduled flights into the Khumbu.

Since 1994, Ang Tsering's jumbo Russian-built Mi-17 helicopters have invaded Khumbu skies. Carrying 8,800 pounds of cargo and twenty-six passengers wedged into jump seats around the sides, they land at Lukla as well as at the tiny airstrip above 12,000 feet at Shyangboche, halfway between Namche and Khumjung. Suitable

(above) TENGBOCHE MONASTERY WITH AMA DABLAM RISING BEHIND; *(right)* TOURISTS DEPARTING KHUMBU FOR KATHMANDU BY HELICOPTER INSTEAD OF WALKING BACK TO LUKLA.

for small STOL planes, the airstrip was contrived to provide access to the Everest View Hotel, a place for people with more money than time, who would rather not make the walk from Lukla.

Mountaineering expeditions used to start at Lukla with at least 300 porters. Now all the gear lands at Shyangboche, and everything and everyone also flies out from there. The porters and the teashops and lodges along the Lukla-Namche trail are losing business. Many people in Khumbu share Sona Hishi's concern: "The zopkios almost losing their transportation job. The rich people more rich and poor people going to be more poor."

Barely visible from the hotel, some fifteen air miles away, the summit pyramid of Everest protrudes above the Nuptse-Lhotse wall, recognizable as much by the plume of wind-driven snow tearing off the summit ridge as by its triangle of darkness. The banner cloud is a sign of the ferocious gales that batter the peak, strong enough to knock people off their feet. It is the jet stream blowing the snow sideways at more than seventy miles per hour.

From the hotel overlook the landscape falls away to the junction of the Dudh Kosi and Imja Khola rivers 2,000 feet below. On a wooded promontory above the confluence stands the Tengboche Monastery, the spiritual heart and religious headquarters of the Khumbu. Off to the right, at the head of the gorge of the Dudh Kosi, Ama Dablam rears up, jabbing the sky with its thumb of sheer ice and rock.

Inside, the hotel appears virtually deserted, suggesting perhaps that Khumbu is not ready for large, pricey lodgings. Ang Tsering sees it differently. With the help of Belgian and local investors, he is building a large hotel in Khumjung.

Mixed blessing though it may be, the new prosperity does not seem to have weakened the strong sense of Sherpa identity. Typical of successful Khumjung-born residents of Kathmandu, Ang Tsering retains his ties with the Khumbu and shows great loyalty to the community. Like many, he returns with his family during the summer festival and wedding season, when the monsoon calls a halt to trekking and mountaineering. He looks forward to the family get-togethers and large social gatherings and has taken a turn along with other villagers as sponsor of the annual Dumje festival to provide the food and drink for the whole village on this merry five-day carnival event. "We are still part of Khumjung," Ang Tsering declares.

Likewise, Mingma Norbu, the urbane executive with the World Wildlife Fund, also wants to be associated with Khumbu. "If I weren't, I would feel exiled from Sherpa society."

Dr. Sally McDonald, during her two years at the Khunde Hospital, was a glad witness to this phenomenon: "We have seen more and more of the urban elite taking on responsibilities in their native communities," she says. "Several Kathmandu Sherpas contributed a lot of money and effort to help restore the Thami monastery. Another group has started to participate in the Khumjung School Committee." And while working on his Ph.D., Lhakpa Norbu helped the villagers in the Thami Valley identify five priority community development projects, four of which have already been funded and enacted.

The Sherpa community also rallied to support the reconstruction of the revered Tengboche Monastery, which burned down in a devastating fire on January 19, 1989. Precious old scriptures, statues, woodcarvings, and murals were lost. With the help of Hillary and the Himalayan Trust, the Sir Edmund Hillary Foundation, the American Himalayan Foundation, and many national and international donors, Tengboche was rebuilt and consecrated on its wooded hill in September 1993.

In fact, not only has the monastery been restored, but a Sherpa cultural center at Tengboche is now on the drawing boards. Working with the abbot, Swiss architect Michael W. Schmitz, a devout Buddhist employed by the monastery, has produced The Tengboche Development Plan. Written after consulting with the monks, lodge managers, park personnel, tourists, porters, and trekking leaders, the proposal stresses that, in the face of rapid changes in Sherpa life, a cultural center "could give the existing Sherpa community a sense of self-respect to carry on."

In addition to creating a cultural repository, the development plan also covers other areas of need. Entry fees to the center,

THE SHERPA COMMUNITY ALSO RALLIED TO SUPPORT THE RECONSTRUC-
TION OF THE REVERED TENGBOCHE MONASTERY, WHICH BURNED DOWN
IN A DEVASTATING FIRE ON JANUARY 19, 1989. . . .WITH THE HELP OF
HILLARY AND THE HIMALAYAN TRUST, THE SIR EDMUND HILLARY
FOUNDATION, THE AMERICAN HIMALAYAN FOUNDATION, AND MANY
NATIONAL AND INTERNATIONAL DONORS, TENGBOCHE WAS REBUILT AND
CONSECRATED ON ITS WOODED HILL IN SEPTEMBER 1993.

(left) LAMA STUDENTS WALKING TO CLASSES AT TENGBOCHE MONASTERY; *(above)*
YOUNG LAMA, MINGMA NORBU SHERPA'S NEPHEW, A STUDENT AT TENGBOCHE.

. . . a cultural center "could give the existing Sherpa community a sense of self-respect to carry on. We need a meditation center," says Schmitz, "and most importantly we need water. The monastery has no toilets."

(left) YOUNG LAMAS IN CLASSROOM RECITING BUDDHIST PRAYERS; (above) LARGER-THAN-LIFE BUDDHA IN GOMPA AT TENGBOCHE MONASTERY; (lower left) HILLARY WITH LAMA AT KHUNDE MONASTERY.

for example, could help finance the cost of running the monastery as well as help protect the local environment. The plan makes a plea to improve the facilities for the monks, as well. "We need a meditation center," says Schmitz, "and most importantly we need water. The monastery has no toilets."

Schmitz's report also seeks support for the monastery school at Tengboche, the only such school in Khumbu. Without the stimulus and inspiration from this wellspring of Khumbu Buddhism, the report maintains, "the survival of Sherpa culture is questionable." Like many Sherpas, His Holiness Ngawang Tenzin Zangbu, the reincarnate abbot of Tengboche, is deeply concerned about preserving native culture and traditions. Normally called the Tengboche Rimpoche, he actively pursues his own fund-raising efforts and also is serving as a teacher and counselor on topics as varied as health,

politics, and naming children born in the district. A reincarnation of Lama Gulo, the monk who founded the monastery in 1916, the abbot is referred to as Rimpoche (*rim poche*—precious jewel), rather than by his name. He aroused people's attention as a young boy in Namche when he spoke about his former home in Tengboche. The boy's lineage was immediately proved genuine when he was able to pick out the monk's clothes and possessions from a mixed pile, thus recognizing objects from a former life.

Sent to be educated in Tibetan monasteries, the Rimpoche returned to Tengboche in 1956, serving not only as its abbot but as overseer of all the Sherpa gompas in Nepal. These days, when he is not on a lengthy meditation retreat, he personally sees more than forty people a day at the monastery—receiving mountaineers, businessmen, nuns, porters, and tourists in a small room behind the main temple. Because of his activist spirit, a departure from the more traditional monastic interests of an abbot, his critics call him "too much of a politician."

Indeed, the Rimpoche had the subtle, appraising look of a diplomat as he waited for Schmitz to translate his remarks spoken in Nepali. He admitted to certain advantages from all the tourism in Khumbu. It has kept many Sherpas at home who would otherwise have migrated to Kathmandu, he pointed out. And because they have more money now, Sherpas are petitioning Tengboche with more requests for monks to come to their houses to read the sacred texts.

(above) HIS HOLINESS ADDRESSING A GATHERING AT TENGBOCHE MONASTERY WITH SIR EDMUND AND LADY JUNE SEATED BEHIND; *(right)* DAWA TSERING SHERPA PLACING FRESH PRAYER FLAGS ON ROOF OF HIS HOME IN KHUNDE.

Nevertheless, the Tengboche Rimpoche from time to time voices pessimism that Sherpa culture can successfully survive this new affluence.

"It is not that materialism necessarily violates Buddhist principles," says His Holiness. "What is much more important is a commitment to good deeds and benefiting others rather than focusing only on oneself, one's family, and one's career. Helping the community is a very positive way of earning credit for a good karma."

In Sherpa eyes, a life well lived is one that has accumulated religious merit for rewards in the next reincarnation. When, for example, Ang Tsering supplies rice, lentils, sugar, and tea to the 180 or so monks and nuns in the district, he is storing up merit in a time-honored, traditional Tibetan-Buddhist way, and supporting the brotherhood of monks is a particularly worthy act.

Perhaps this simple faith in the efficacy of good deeds lies at the heart of the Sherpa character—the source of the loyalty, integrity, and personal warmth that so endeared these people to Hillary and the other early mountaineers. "That awareness of karma stays strongly in the Sherpa's mind on a day-to-day level," affirms Mingma Norbu.

Sherpas also still cling to what Sona Hishi calls "the old things of personal life." When death strikes, the family holds the same series of funeral rites. Before the cremation, monks arrive in the house to recite the Tibetan Book of the Dead. The monks sit cross-legged, rocking back and forth to the rapid rhythm of their prayers. Clashing cymbals, drums, and trumpets accompany the droning voices, which sound like the distant rumble of thunder. After the cremation, the monks recite texts that guide the soul of the departed through Bardo, a dreamlike realm between death and rebirth. The prayers bolster the soul on its passage through this limbo toward its next reincarnation by reminding it that the monsters en route, like all phenomena of existence, are mere shadows and illusions.

Other beliefs and rituals have also survived. The smoke and scent of burning juniper still bless each new building. Most houses still have a chapel, a prominent side-room called the *Lhakhang*, where a scarlet-and-gilt shrine is elaborately decorated with paintings in which every design has meaning. Its shelves and niches gleam with silver censers and butter lamps and golden Buddha images. High on a central shelf sits a framed portrait of the Dalai Lama, the exiled god-king of the Tibetans.

"If you go to any Sherpa house, you will see they still worship every morning, pouring fresh water into seven bowls. Water, a symbol of purity, serves as an offering to Buddha," said Mingma.

"If you go to any Sherpa house, you will see they still worship every morning, pouring fresh water into seven bowls. Water, a symbol of purity, serves as an offering to Buddha." —Mingma Norbu Sherpa

(far left) FINGER CYMBALS USED IN RELIGIOUS CEREMONIES;
(left) BUDDHIST PRAYERS ON PRAYER FLAGS; (right) LAMA
PLAYING HORN DURING MANI RIMDU CEREMONY AT THAMI
MONASTERY.

But while inherited values and traditions remain, fundamental change is taking place. The transformation of Khumbu is not just a matter of Gortex jackets and metal roofs. Once, Sherpas lived in a basically open, egalitarian society, where everyone was more or less of equal wealth and experience. The gap between the big traders of the past and other Sherpas was not that great; after all, nearly every family had somebody who was doing a little business trading on the side. Seventy years ago the trader's house wouldn't have been all that different from a poor farmer's. Now a new class of people with radically different experiences and levels of wealth has suddenly emerged.

Sherpa society has also fractured into different levels of experience. The children of the wealthy go to private schools in Kathmandu, where the medium of instruction is either Nepali or English. Though these children may visit the ancestral village once or twice a year, they are growing up speaking only a little bit of Sherpa—much to the chagrin of their wealthy parents. "Still we are trying to teach them some attachment to Sherpa culture," sighs Ang Rita.

In the Hillary-assisted government schools, where the medium of instruction is Nepali, the only language classes have been English . . . until recently, that is. Now the Khumjung school has started teaching Tibetan. And at the Junbesi school, where the headmaster is one of the very few Sherpas still in the school system, Sherpa is

(below) VENDORS WITH THEIR PRODUCE AT THE WEEKLY SATURDAY MARKET IN NAMCHE BAZAR; (right) SHERPA BOY WITH BOOKS AT KHUMJUNG SCHOOL.

(above) TEMBA SHERPA PAINTING LOCAL SCENES IN TIBETAN STYLE TO SELL TO TOURISTS; (right) ANG PHURBA SERVING TEA AT HIS LODGE TO MINGMA NORBU AND CHANDRA GURUNG.

now being taught with textbooks that have transliterated the language into the Tibetan alphabet and written it down for the first time. But the headmaster's own son, who attends college in Kathmandu and is fluent in English, did not understand the words of a traditional Sherpa song sung at a community celebration in honor of Hillary.

Another troubling change, says Kami Temba, the former health assistant at the Khunde Hospital, is the changing status of Sherpa women. Traditionally a Sherpani was a self-reliant, equal partner of her husband and an assertive member of society. "In the old days, men and women did some of the same work. Both went on trading trips to Tibet and carried the same loads. Women were also important in farming and animal husbandry," says Kami Temba, holding

144

his two-year-old daughter in his lap. "Many women were also enterprising traders and money-lenders.

"But tourism is a male-oriented industry," he explains, "and so women have lost much of their income generating capacity. Society always regards those who make more money as more desirable, so men have increased their status at the expense of women. If girls were given more educational opportunities, they would also make good trekking guides—or teachers or electricians."

In their complex struggle to balance old ways and new and to resist assimilation into the Hindu majority, educated Sherpas seem to worry most about preserving their cultural heritage. But rather than an ethnic angst, their concern reflects a determination to remain distinctly Sherpa.

"Government policy discourages holding onto our ways," says Mingma. "You have to speak Nepali. You have to be a Nepali. But on the whole, people like myself have become more aware of our culture because we have been away from the Khumbu. Mixing with other cultures has reinforced our sense of identity because I see that Sherpa culture has a lot to offer."

As Fisher observes in his insightful book, "Sherpas are so massively reinforced at every point for being Sherpa, they have every reason not only to stay Sherpa but even to flaunt their Sherpahood. One might say that tourists pay Sherpas in part for being Sherpa, or at least for performing the role that accords with the popular image."

Mingma endorses Fisher's assessment. "He is correct. If you observe carefully, in his heart a Sherpa always remains a Sherpa. Whether he is a pilot or a porter, whether he is in Kathmandu or Thami, he is a real Buddhist Sherpa," says Mingma. "After all, these days it is chic to be Sherpa."

(above) KHUMJUNG VILLAGERS IN CEREMONIAL DRESS FOR OSHO CEREMONY TO BLESS NEWLY PLANTED POTATO FIELDS; (right) MANAGER OF KHUMJUNG BAKERY SLICING A FRESH PIE FOR TOURISTS.

Time seems to be on the Sherpas' side—at least ever since 1960, when Hillary asked his friends in Khumjung, "What can we do for you and your village?"

As a result, the Hillary schools and Hillary's steadfast endorsement of Sherpa aspirations have made it possible for the Sherpas to remain in charge of their destiny. Those with the talents for trade and business have been able to chart a new course in these times of transition. Education has opened new vistas for others.

Nowhere in Khumbu do you sense the despair of people exploited by fortune hunters or facing absorption by outsiders. Instead, Sherpas take pride in their skills and accomplishments. Sherpas face the future with confidence, and, as anthropologist Fisher and Mingma point out, Sherpa cultural identity is stronger than ever.

When people wonder about the role Hillary has played in the fortunes of the Sherpa people, they might turn to Fisher's assessment: "The schools are the crucial link between tradition and modernity because they have enabled Sherpas to exploit the forces of change. . . . Having successfully met the modern world on their own terms, the educated Sherpas have the cultural self-confidence to intensify their ethnic identity."

But Mingma Norbu Sherpa's testimonial is more personal— and certainly as compelling: "Before, a Sherpa could be a potato farmer or an expedition porter. That was it. Now that has changed. Because of Sir Ed a twelve-year-old boy or girl can say, 'My life can be different.' Sir Ed has allowed the Sherpas to help themselves. Sherpas are acquiring a new mindset. We are saying, 'I can do this.'"

Perpetuating the Hillary Legacy

Mingma Norbu Sherpa, a slight and slender man with a reserved, unassuming manner, belongs to the first generation of Sherpas who took advantage of the opportunities made possible by the creation of Hillary's village schools. A number of these "Hillary students" have gone on to become doctors, teachers, executives, and wealthy businessmen. Others, empowered by education, have made the most of Khumbu's new tourist economy and have prospered by owning and operating lodges, shops, and teahouses.

Mingma, however, perhaps more than anyone else, embodies the virtues of doing things the Hillary way. And as an executive with the World Wildlife Fund (WWF), the largest privately supported international conservation organization in the world, Mingma has taken Hillary's vision for Khumbu as his goal for other remote areas of the world: The unique flora and fauna of these remote areas, and their often remarkable indigenous peoples, must be protected from the voracious appetites of increased world populations.

Mingma definitely represents a new breed—the suburban Sherpa. He commutes from his home in Virginia to Washington, D.C., to his job with WWF. A dedicated conservationist, Mingma had been the first Sherpa Chief Warden at Sagarmatha (Mount Everest) National Park in Khumbu, where he was in a position to deal with

the environmental issues that deeply concerned Hillary: the deforested slopes and the accumulation of trash on the mountain and in the region.

Before going to work for WWF, he had made a name for himself as one of the founders of Nepal's 1,000-square-mile Annapurna Conservation Area Project (ACAP), a new model for conservation funded by WWF and since duplicated all over the world. Today Mingma is WWF's Director of Conservation for the Asia and Pacific Region and runs the WWF programs in the Eastern Himalayas, working with the governments of China, India, Pakistan, Bhutan, Nepal, and Myanmar to help local communities manage their own natural resources through projects that integrate conservation with economic programs that meet local needs.

Known by its panda logo, WWF, since its founding in 1961, has worked in hundreds of remote locations to protect wildlife and wild lands. But since the mid-1980s WWF has evolved a more complicated strategy in environmental management than merely protecting single endangered species in ghetto-like reserves. Instead, this new approach creates "conservation areas," like the pioneer ACAP in the Annapurna region, which consider the needs of people as well as those of plants and animals.

"In developing countries, like Nepal, you cannot set up national parks that just drive people away or deprive them of resources," asserts Mingma. "Saving nature need not take place at the expense of people."

In fact, Mingma and his colleagues at WWF recognize that unless the projects or programs win the hearts and minds of the people, conservation has little chance of enduring achievement. "We call the concept 'conservation with a human face,'" he says.

While Mingma has been involved with WWF's earliest efforts to promote this concept, he is quick to credit Hillary's work as his inspiration. After all, it was Hillary who so effectively and resolutely involved the Sherpas in his own endeavors—and who also played such a crucial role in the young Mingma's education.

(pg. 148) MINGMA NORBU SHERPA IN SAGARMATHA NATIONAL PARK WITH AMA DABLAM IN BACKGROUND; (pg. 149–crescent) ENTRANCE TO PARK; (above) MINGMA WITH SEEDLING; (top right) MINGMA WITH SHERPANI WHO MAKES BRIQUETTES FROM RECYCLED MATERIAL WHICH REPLACES NEED FOR FIREWOOD; (right) REPRESENTATIVE OF WWF INSPECTING CARROTS GROWN BY SHERPA; (below) FAMILIAR PANDA LOGO OF WWF.

"In developing countries, like Nepal, you cannot set up national parks that just drive people away or deprive them of resources. Saving nature need not take place at the expense of people."
—*Mingma Norbu*

(left) HILLARY ENJOYING LIGHT MOMENT WITH NIMA TASHI, MINGMA NORBU'S GRANDFATHER, IN 1985; *(above)* CLASSROOM AT KHUMJUNG SCHOOL; *(below)* HILLARY PLANTING A SEEDLING IN SAGARMATHA NATIONAL PARK.

"For the first time I became aware of how Hillary's funding and support were making a difference in the lives of the Sherpa people."—Mingma Norbu

There were about fifty children in that first class in the Khumjung School, approximately twenty of whom progressed together through the fifth grade, which was as far as they could go in Khumbu. Mingma was one of three top students in the class selected to go for further study in western Nepal, and from there he went on to high school and two years of college in Kathmandu.

While still a student in Kathmandu, Mingma and some of the other scholarship boys were invited by Hillary to come along on a school-building project in 1972.

"It was an interesting eye-opener for me," he recalls. "For the first time I became aware of how Hillary's funding and support were making a difference in the lives of the Sherpa people."

In many ways Hillary became something of a father figure for the twenty-year-old student, for Mingma's father had died in 1971 while working as a high-altitude porter on a Japanese expedition to Mount Everest. But for the precocious country boy, Hillary was also a role model, mentor, and hero whose grass-roots approach in matters of government, management, and development set an example for Mingma that was as much a part of his education as his schooling.

Mingma's career took a significant turn—and maintained its Hillary connection—with the establishment of Sagarmatha National Park. When, thanks to Hillary's lobbying, a group of New Zealand foresters and Nepalese ecologists was sent to Khumbu to do a feasibility study on the proposed park, Mingma, not yet a college graduate, was assigned to accompany the mission as translator.

"My participation must have been Hillary's idea," says Mingma. "It was Hillary's way of involving Sherpas in the park, right from the start."

Moreover, when the task force recommended that the local people should be involved in the management of the park, the idea clearly bore the stamp of Hillary's thinking and characteristic approach. The proposal was innovative, even revolutionary, at the time, but it was bought by the Nepalese government. As a result, three candidates from Khumbu were selected for training in natural resource and park management. Of course, Mingma was one of the three. In 1976 he departed for Lincoln College in Christchurch, New Zealand, on a four-year scholarship obtained with Hillary's help.

In early 1980, at age twenty-six, Mingma, equipped with a B.A. in forestry and park management, was appointed junior ranger at Sagarmatha in charge of forestry and outdoor activities. Six months later he took over from a New Zealander as the first Sherpa Chief Warden. The country boy from the Khumjung School was running this great Himalayan park.

But his debut was a baptism by fire, for the local Sherpas had serious misgivings about the park and its regulations—especially

(top left) FIRST SHERPA WARDEN OF SAGARMATHA NATIONAL PARK, MINGMA NORBU, AT AGE TWENTY-SIX IN A 1983 PHOTO; (above) VIEW OF SAGARMATHA NATIONAL PARK HEADQUARTERS AND SURROUNDING SCENERY; (bottom right) WICKER CARRYING BASKETS IN FRONT OF WOODPILE OUTSIDE SHERPA LODGE.

those relating to tree-cutting. As Mingma explains, when a Sherpa son is born, the family has to cut a large, straight juniper tree to put up a prayer flag. Green wood is also necessary to repair Sherpa houses and for a Sherpa cremation.

From Mingma's perspective, of course, the problem was exacerbated by the tremendous demand for firewood from the deluge of tourists, all of whom craved the experience of sitting around the traditional campfire. So, not only did Sherpas still need wood for their own purposes, they had also become accustomed to a profitable business in selling it to tourists.

Such was the local opposition to the laws against cutting green wood that, by the time Mingma arrived in Khumbu, it was estimated that more forest had been cut down in the initial years of the park's establishment than ever before. The Sherpas thought they wouldn't be able to get wood anymore, so they basically were stockpiling as much as they could.

The new park warden soon realized that distrust and misunderstanding created much of the Sherpa cynicism toward the park and much of the resistance to controls. Sagarmatha was not popular with the locals because they had not been consulted. Unlike Hillary's projects, which were conceived and conducted in close liaison with the community, management at the park was too top-down. Plans and projects were being hatched in distant offices. Decisions seemed to be implemented arbitrarily.

"The basic problem was that the Sherpas were not aware of the philosophy of the park and did not know why the park was created," says Mingma.

"Another tactic during my tenure was to secure the blessing of the Rimpoche—the high lama—of the Tengboche Monastery. For example, at a reforestation project, we would have the Rimpoche sanctify the area for the planting of the first tree. That way the local people would be inclined to respect the area."
—Mingma Norbu

(top left) MINGMA AT PARK HEAD-QUARTERS WITH 15-YEAR-OLD SEEDLINGS; *(top right)* HIS HOLINESS OF TENGBOCHE MONASTERY, WHO HAS BEEN VERY SUPPORTIVE OF MINGMA IN REFORESTA-TION AND OTHER PROJECTS; *(left)* LHAKPA NORBU, WHO RECEIVED A PH.D. IN FORESTRY.

His top priority, then, was to teach the Sherpas to appreciate the importance of the park and to believe in reforestation. To further understanding, he launched a conservation-education program in the local schools, and he revived the indigenous forest management system, bending the rules a little bit by hiring community-appointed "forest guardians" to work for the park. Traditionally, these *shingi nawas* protected the forest from unauthorized cutting and were responsible for controlling its use. Hillary's Himalayan Trust helped Mingma with his plan by paying the salaries of these unofficial wardens.

"One of my major achievements was linking this traditional system of forest management with the park's administration," says Mingma. "Another tactic during my tenure was to secure the bless-ing of the Rimpoche—the high lama—of the Tengboche Monastery. For example, at a reforestation project, we would have the Rimpoche sanctify the area for the planting of the first tree. That way the local people would be inclined to respect the area."

These emerging strategies and the lessons learned at Sagarmatha did double duty in 1985, when Mingma was asked to become one of three principal investigators hired to determine the status of Nepal's 1,000-square-mile Annapurna region, which had a native population close to 80,000 and trekkers numbering an overwhelming 25,000 a year. Their decisions would shape the future for the dramatically scenic area. The invitation to Mingma to participate in the study came from Nepal's King Mahendra Trust for Conservation and from WWF, which funded the study.

"I picked Mingma. I hired him sight unseen," says Dr. Bruce W. Bunting, WWF's vice president for Asia. "But I knew about him, and I read about him. He had just finished his masters degree in natural resource management. And Mingma had the highest recommendation anyone could have—from Sir Edmund Hillary, a man who has served on the board of WWF International for many years and has been an active supporter of WWF New Zealand and WWF in Nepal.

(top left) MINGMA INSPECTING BEANS COOKED IN A SOLAR CONTAINER; (right) SIGNS IN NAMCHE DIRECTING TOURISTS TO VARIOUS LOCATIONS; (left) SHERPANI GROWING LETTUCE AND OTHER VEGETABLES IN GREENHOUSE.

"The whole issue of people living inside a park was a problem Mingma had already dealt with," says Bunting. "Mingma contributed a very specific point of view—that the best way to protect resources was to let people retain ownership and responsibility." It was vintage Hillary. The concept that local populations have a right and responsibility to be actively involved in making decisions regarding their future would become a prevailing principle throughout Mingma's career. Mingma was bringing the Hillary legacy into a larger arena.

One of the project's proudest accomplishments was determining that the entry fees would stay in the area for conservation activities and that the local people would be involved in deciding where this tourist money should be spent. These days the $15 fee, multiplied by 48,000 visitors, generates $700,000 per year—money that is plowed back into projects like setting up kerosene depots and training lodge owners and operators in food preparation and other innkeeper skills.

159

"ACAP was unique," says Bunting. "Since then it has become a model for conservation and has been the subject of numerous chapters and books. These days involving local residents in the planning and management of protected areas is a very big thing in the conservation lexicon."

Initially, WWF provided only the money that funded ACAP. Now it is also providing the philosophy—Hillary's living legacy that both Mingma and WWF share.

Although as an executive of WWF Mingma is heavily involved in wide-ranging projects in the Eastern Himalayas—from a tri-national peace park that straddles the borders of China, India, and Nepal to protecting the highly endangered snow leopard—his Sherpa

homeland is not neglected. As a national park, and not a conservation area, Sagarmatha is regulated and managed by the government of Nepal. But WWF, on Mingma's initiative, is supporting an agro-forestry program in the Pharak district, just south of the park. The Pharak area, not as engaged in tourism as Khumbu, will benefit from growing fruit trees, firewood, and vegetables to supply the villages to the north.

Of course, the project is managed locally—by the Sagarmatha Pollution Control Committee (SPCC), which had been set up with the help of the WWF in 1991 to tackle the trash left in Khumbu by trekkers and climbing expeditions. The pollution, labeled the world's highest garbage dump, was a problem the Sherpas themselves wanted to solve, and Mingma responded with suggestions of what WWF might do to help. Here, once again, Hillary's principle of local control was at work.

And when Mingma shows up in Khumbu, he elicits the outpouring of affection that recalls the visits of Hillary. As Mingma's friend, Bunting, reports, "The villagers turn out and line the trails. They love and admire him incredibly."

Mingma is the local boy perpetuating the legacy of the burrah sahib. He simply does what the Sherpas want him to do.

(top) MINGMA NORBU CONGRATULATING HILLARY AT A BLACK TIE AWARDS DINNER IN TORONTO, CANADA; *(top right)* MEMBERS OF THE LOCAL SHINGINAWA GROUP AT LOCAL SHERPA HOME; *(lower right)* MINGMA BEING GREETED AND REVERED FOR HIS COMMITMENT AND DEDICATION; *(above)* GRAPH SHOWING LEVEL OF TRASH CLEARING; *(middle)* TRASH-BURNING PROJECT OUTSIDE KHUNDE/KHUMJUNG.

MINGMA IS THE LOCAL BOY PERPETUATING THE LEGACY OF THE BURRAH SAHIB. WHEN HE SHOWS UP IN KHUMBU, HE ELICITS THE OUTPOURING OF AFFECTION THAT RECALLS THE VISITS OF HILLARY. AS MINGMA'S FRIEND, BUNTING, REPORTS, "THE VILLAGERS TURN OUT AND LINE THE TRAILS. THEY LOVE AND ADMIRE HIM INCREDIBLY."

In 1961, when forty-one-year-old Sir Edmund Hillary went to the offices of the *World Book Encyclopedia* in Chicago to seek financial support for a scientific expedition to the Himalayas, he was an international celebrity—a mountaineer, Antarctic explorer, lecturer, and conquering hero feted by presidents, prime ministers, and kings. The Chicago executives awaiting Hillary expected him to arrive with an entourage of lawyers and accountants. But the businessmen were in for a big surprise: fame and knighthood had done nothing to alter Hillary's modest, unassuming manner. The meeting, as recounted by one of the executives, is reported in Pat Booth's 1993 biography *Edmund Hillary, The Life of a Legend*:

> *Then in comes this tall guy, by himself, with his hair all over the place and carrying an old briefcase held together with string. Well, that threw us right from the start. And then when we came to the bit where we asked how much he would like for himself he says: "Well, on an expedition we don't usually take any money for ourselves." We didn't know whether he meant it. For a bit, we thought he might just be the coolest cat we'd ever met. Then, we began to feel sorry for him. We felt we had to help this guy—force him to take the money.*

But those who know Hillary also know that his high principles and modest, unassuming style mask a legendary determination. The drive, inner toughness, and tenacity that took him to the top of the world have also kept him in dogged pursuit of projects to help the Sherpa people. Although he is quick to point out that "fund-raising is not dear to my heart," the aversion has not deterred him from spending part of each year for more than three decades doing just that, all for the sake of giving back to those less fortunate than he.

The money that finances his Sherpa projects comes not from corporate slush funds but from ordinary people who respond to Hillary's low-key charisma and his deep affection for the Sherpa. "He is as pleased when a group of children raises thirty-eight dollars, as when he receives a check for $150," says his friend and director of the Canadian Sir Edmund Hillary Foundation, Zeke O'Connor.

(pg.162) STUDENTS OF THAMI SCHOOL GREETING SIR EDMUND WITH KATAS AND SWEETS ON HIS ANNUAL VISIT TO THEIR VILLAGE IN KHUMBU; (top left) DAWA TSERING REVIEWING PROJECT PLANS WITH HILLARY IN KHUNDE; (top right) CHILDREN LEANING OUT WINDOW AT BENI SCHOOL IN SOLO TO VIEW HILLARY AS HE ARRIVES FOR A VISIT; (right) PHOTOS FROM NEW ZEALAND NEWSPAPERS PASTED ON WALLS OF KHUNDE HOME OF MINGMA TSERING AND ANG DOOLI; (left) HILLARY AND HIS WIFE, JUNE, FOLLOWING A TRAILSIDE PETITION MEETING FOR A NEW SCHOOL ROOF IN KHUMBU.

Hillary's lectures are sincere, forthright, and unemotional, though often leavened with his wry, self-mocking humor. When a fan admired his modesty, Hillary's comeback was characteristic: "I have much to be modest about." The reply—smooth, without being slick—suggests some of Hillary's endearing charm.

But make no mistake: on the issues dear to him, Hillary remains outspoken and uncompromising, with an ingrained sense of fairness and justice, and he has used his celebrity to make his voice heard nationally and internationally. In 1969, a time of racial apartheid in South Africa, he deplored the fact that no New Zealand rugby players had "seen fit to put their principles before a free trip and a dollop of glory." He has also publicly chastised New Zealand's Prime Minister and his colleagues for political "expediency" and double-dealing.

Perhaps even more offensive to Hillary's moral compass than political corruption is the grinding poverty in the Third World, where a vast gap separates the rich and poor. Over four decades he has raised the question again and again, repeatedly scolding the government of New Zealand for not providing more foreign aid for the very needy.

Although a certain righteous indignation impels Hillary into action, he never assumes the sanctimonious manner of a crusader or zealot who feels he has a monopoly on truth. As he observes to biographer Booth, "I don't by any means have all the answers to

(left) HILLARY PASSING A MANI WALL RESPECTFULLY TO HIS RIGHT DURING ONE OF HIS FINAL TREKS IN THE KHUMBU; *(above)* HILLARY WITH FORMER KHUMJUNG SCHOOL STUDENTS ANG RITA AND LHAKPA NORBU, LEFT, AND CURRENT SCHOLARSHIP STUDENT, RIGHT.

As his lifelong friend,
George Lowe, points
out, Hillary is "an or-
dinary man who is at
the same time a most
extraordinary man."

these problems, but I do believe that we human beings have a right and duty to speak out, to express our concerns on these matters."

As his lifelong friend, George Lowe, points out, Hillary is "an ordinary man who is at the same time a most extraordinary man." Indeed, Hillary's very ordinariness makes his achievements so memorable. In a world that pursues money, power, and influence, Hillary remains utterly unspoiled by his fame. His celebrity is no more than a means to an end: "If that one day on Everest allows me to do what I do, so be it."

To see Hillary move among the Sherpas is to see a man borne aloft by love and respect. The people regard him as a savior, as a devoted father who has provided them with an education, well-paying jobs, and longer and healthier lives. And by returning to the Solu-Khumbu year after year to see what must be done, he has set an example for mankind. "Just an ordinary chap" who derives satisfaction from giving people in the distant Himalayas a "bit of a hand," Hillary serves as a model of right behavior. His lifetime of compassion and dedication make him a true champion and hero.

(above) STUDENT PRESENTING HILLARY WITH KATAS AT KHUMJUNG SCHOOL; (right) MOONLIT PEAKS OF KANTEGA, LEFT, AND TAMSERKU TOWERING ABOVE THE KHUMBU VILLAGES OF KHUNDE/KHUMJUNG.

THE PEOPLE REGARD HIM AS A SAVIOR, AS A DEVOTED FATHER WHO HAS PROVIDED THEM WITH AN EDUCATION, WELL-PAYING JOBS, AND LONGER AND HEALTHIER LIVES. AND BY RETURNING TO THE SOLU-KHUMBU YEAR AFTER YEAR TO SEE WHAT MUST BE DONE, HE HAS SET AN EXAMPLE FOR MANKIND.

The Himalayan Trust

I first visited the Khumbu area on the south side of Mt. Everest in 1951 and developed a warm respect and affection for the Sherpa people who lived there. Their life was a tough and hardy one but they had a most vigorous sense of humour. It was impossible not to like their cheerfulness and generosity.

Over the next ten years, I developed many Sherpa friends and became aware of the things they lacked in their rugged existence—no schooling for their children and no medical treatment for the ill. I often felt there was much we could do to help them but never got beyond the stage of talking and dreaming.

Finally in 1961, in response to a serious request from my Sherpa friends, I raised the necessary funds and we constructed the Khumjung School—the first permanent school in the Mt. Everest area. With a group of my New Zealand mountaineering friends, we established the Himalayan Trust as a fundraising body and to supervise and plan the growing number of projects.

From every direction petitions were presented for schools, hospitals, medical clinics, bridges and fresh water pipelines, and in cooperation with the Sherpas we went ahead and built them. We even constructed several steep mountain airfields. To help with finance, we established other foundations in the U.S.A. and Canada and obtained financial assistance too in Australia and the United Kingdom. Now we have been responsible for establishing more than twenty-six schools, two hospitals, twelve medical clinics and many bridges and water supplies.

We feel that the finance we have raised for these projects has been money well spent. It has brought education and health care to hundreds—indeed thousands—of these worthy hill people. The work must be continued, we believe, for this is what the Sherpas want.
—*Sir Edmund Hillary*

For further information on The Himalayan Trust, please address correspondence to any of the chapters listed below.

SIR EDMUND HILLARY, CHAIRMAN
Himalayan Trust
278A Remuera Road
Auckland 5
New Zealand

MR. LARRY WITHERBEE, PRESIDENT
The Hillary Foundation
814 Saddlewood Drive
Glen Ellyn, Illinois 60137
United States

MR. ZEKE O'CONNOR, PRESIDENT
The Sir Edmund Hillary Foundation
222 Jarvis Street
4th Floor HQB
Toronto, Ontario
Canada

GEORGE LOWE C. NZ.M., O.B.E.
Sir Edmund Hillary Himalayan Trust
Lowecroft, Plains Lane
Blackbrook, Belper, Derby DE56 2DD
England

THE EXCELLENCE FOUNDATION
WAS CREATED WITH THE FOLLOWING MISSION:

*To acknowledge achievements of excellence in all areas,
to inspire the achievement of excellence, and
to apply the knowledge attained through the achievement of excellence
to a broader public benefit.*

THE FOUNDATION SEEKS TO ACCOMPLISH THIS MISSION BY EDUCATING THE PUBLIC
ABOUT THE ACHIEVEMENT OF EXCELLENCE IN VARIOUS PROFESSIONS OR ENDEAVORS,
AND BY PRESENTING SPECIFIC EXAMPLES OF EXCELLENCE TO PROMOTE LEADERSHIP, COURAGE,
THE SPIRIT OF ADVENTURE, SAFETY, FITNESS, AND HEALTH.

THE EXCELLENCE FOUNDATION
109 West Union Street, Box 379
Manchester, Vermont 05254
802-366-8157 (tel)
802-366-8146 (fax)

⚜ ACKNOWLEDGEMENTS ⚜

For nearly twenty years while this book was in creation, many people have provided unending encouragement to make it a reality. I would like to take this opportunity to express my gratitude to them.

First and foremost my thanks go to Sir Edmund Hillary. Ed has been a dedicated friend since we first met in 1983. He has offered time for interviews, provided personal photographs to help with illustrations, and always welcomed my company on treks. Most important, his remarkable life has been the basis for the creation of this book. I am also indebted to Lady June Hillary for her guidance, support, and friendship, as well as to other members of the Hillary family—including Ed's sister, June Carlisle; his brother, Rex Hillary; and his son, Peter Hillary.

I am indebted to the extraordinary writing talents of author Cynthia Russ Ramsay, whose exquisite text offers the reader wonderful insights into Hillary's life, the Sherpa world, and its magnificent people.

Deep gratitude also goes to George Lowe, one of the original members of the 1953 Mt. Everest Expedition. George has provided invaluable insights into details of the expedition and also shared personal photographs of the Hillary family which have added much to the visual portrayal of Hillary's life. And I would like to thank both George and his wife, Mary, for their work with the the Sir Edmund Hillary Himalayan Trust in the United Kingdom.

In addition, I would like to thank other Himalayan Trust comrades. Both Larry Witherbee, at the The Hillary Foundation in Chicago, and Zeke O'Connor, at The Sir Edmund Hillary Foundation in Toronto, have been trekking partners over many years, as well as true advisors in the development of the book. Elizabeth Hawley and Ang Rita Sherpa, who manage the Himalayan Trust in Kathmandu, Nepal, are also steadfast friends who have also provided ongoing assistance over many years.

In addition to Ang Rita Sherpa, many other Sherpas have enriched my life with their enduring support and comradeship. In particular, I would like to thank Mingma Norbu Sherpa of the World Wildlife Fund, Lhakpa Norbu Sherpa of the Mountain Institute, Pilot Ang Zangbu Sherpa, and Mingma Gyelzen and Kami Temba, both Sherpa doctors. All were students at the Hillary schools in Solo Khumbu. I also thank my many other Sherpa friends whose friendship I have enjoyed on numerous treks.

My special thanks go to Jane d'Alelio of Ice House Graphics for her extraordinary artistic conceptual vision for the book and the cover, to Dan and Nancy Hutner of the Excellence Foundation, which has provided ongoing support for this project, and to literary agent Gail Ross.

I am enormously grateful to all the people at Lionheart Books: Michael Reagan, Deb Murphy, Paul Wheeler, designer Carley Brown, and editor John Yow. Working with them has been pure joy.

I am also indebted to Joanna Scadden, at the Royal Geographical Society, for her assistance with historical photographs from the 1953 Mt. Everest Expedition, to Louis Plummer and Sidney Brown, at PhotoAssist in Washington, D.C., for their help with illustrations, and to my dear friend, Whitney Stewart, author of the children's book, *Sir Edmund Hillary, To Everest and Beyond,* for her many years of guidance.

Finally this book would never have happened without the enduring support and encouragement of my husband, Douglas Lapp. His faith in me and in the book have sustained me through periods of frustration and guided me to realize my dream.—*Anne Keiser*

⍟ ACKNOWLEDGEMENTS ⍟

I am indebted to many people for helping me to gather and present the written material for this book.

I owe a special debt to photographer, Anne Keiser. Apart from the vivid photographs, which are such a lavish part of the book, Anne's long friendship with Sir Edmund Hillary facilitated many things for me in my research. Anne's other contacts from her numerous trips to Sherpa country were also enormously helpful to me. And without her steadfast determination there would probably be no book, for she set a high goal and then had the faith and determination to reach it.

From the start, the project enjoyed the financial support of The Excellence Foundation, an organization extolling those who use their fame to make extraordinary humanitarian contributions.

I also owe a special debt of gratitude to the many Sherpas who let me tap into their memories. There are too many to list individually, but I would like to especially thank Ang Rita Sherpa, of the Himalayan Trust in Kathmandu, forest ecologist Dr. Lhakpa Norbu Sherpa, Mingma Norbu Sherpa, of the World Wildlife Fund, airline pilot Ang Zangbu Sherpa, and Kami Temba, who is probably a doctor by now rather than a health worker at the Khunde Hospital. They were all gold mines of information, and afterwards the first three people also gave of their time checking the manuscript for accuracy. I am very grateful to all of them.

In addition, I gained especially valuable insights from my interviews with Elizabeth Hawley, a longtime resident of Nepal and a unique source of information on the guiding principles of the Hillary Trust. I also had the benefit of interviews with the abbot of the Tengboche Monastery, the Venerable Ngawang Tenzin Zangbu, and Michael W. Schmitz, a Swiss consultant to the abbot on developing a cultural center at Tengboche.

In helping to edit my manuscript my special thanks go to Robert L. Breeden, a Trustee Emeritus of the National Geographic Society, for his insightful questions, helpful suggestions, and meticulous copyediting. I would also like to thank Lady Hillary, Douglas Lapp, and Nancy Hutner, of the Excellence Foundation, for their careful reading of the manuscript. This is also the place to thank Whitney Stewart for generously making available to me, for background information, the interviews she recorded for her children's book on Hillary. I am also grateful to her for reading the manuscript.

Quotations from Sir Edmund Hillary in the text come from my interview with him in Nepal, from the books he has authored, and from the magazine articles he wrote for the *National Geographic*.

I spent a considerable amount of time with most of the other people cited in the text, but I relied on my reading of James F. Fisher's book, *Sherpas, Reflections on Change in Himalayan Nepal*, to quote the author, and I used the account in the October 1966 issue of the *National Geographic* by the late journalist Desmond Doig as a source for the story in Chapter Two about Khonjo Chhumbi, a village elder, and his landmark journey abroad. I have also benefited from reading Pat Booth's biography, *Edmund Hillary, The Life of a Legend*, and from reading those classics of Himalayan ethnology by Christoph von Fürer-Haimendorf—his three volumes on the Sherpas.

To Sir Edmund Hillary and the Sherpa people, who made this writing venture such a rewarding experience, many thanks.—*Cynthia Russ Ramsay*